Eat Like You Care

An Examination of the Morality of Eating Animals

Gary L. Francione

Anna Charlton

EXEMPLA PRESS

"Exempla" is the plural of "exemplum," or a story, which could be real or fictitious, used to make a moral point. Exemplary literature was a genre that was popular in classical, medieval, and Renaissance literature.

Eat Like You Care Book website
www.EatLikeYouCareBook.com

Authors' website
www.AbolitionistApproach.com

This book is intended to provide accurate information with regards to its subject matter; however, in times of rapid change, ensuring all information provided is entirely accurate and up-to-date at all times is not always possible. Therefore, the authors and publisher accept no responsibility for inaccuracies or omissions and specifically disclaim any liability, loss or risk, personal, professional or otherwise, which may be incurred as a consequence, directly or indirectly, of the use and/or application of any of the contents of this book.

Dedicated to the approximately 57 billion land animals and one trillion aquatic animals we will consume in the next year.

So much suffering.
So much death.
All so unnecessary.
All so wrong.

Contents

Acknowledgments

Thanks to Mariana C. Gonzalez, Aruna Lopez, Linda McKenzie, and Melissa Resnick for their editorial suggestions.

Thanks to Vincent Guihan for designing the cover and to Vincent Guihan, Mariana C. Gonzalez, Foppe de Haan, and Kevin O'Keeffe for assistance in the production process.

Introduction

The number of animals used for food is overwhelming. According to the United Nations Food and Agricultural Organization, humans kill more than 57 billion animals a year for food. One billion is a thousand million. This number does not include the number of fish and other aquatic animals we consume. That number is estimated to be *at the very least* another one trillion. One trillion is a million million.

That's an absolutely staggering amount of suffering and death.

If you are like most people, you like animals. In fact, you may even think of yourself as an "animal lover." But you also probably eat meat, dairy, eggs, and other animal products.

You've thought about this and it has troubled you. You suspect that the process of raising and slaughtering animals is pretty brutal and you aren't sure about how you should respond.

Most of us, when we were children, were horrified to learn that we were eating animals — beings who, at least in an abstract sense, we loved. In order to assure us, our parents told us one story or another, such as that God wanted us to eat animals or that we would be weak and ill if we did not consume animal products, and so we grew comfortable with eating them.

As we got older, we kept our moral quiescence on the matter by convincing ourselves of the many excuses that are explored in this book. The prevalence of these excuses, together with the fact that they don't really satisfy us, establishes very clearly that we know something is not right here.

And now there is a move afoot to address our concerns by offering us "free-range" this, "cage-free" that, and a whole range of other "happy" meat and animal products. Is this the answer? Is the answer to continue consuming animal products that are supposedly "humanely" produced? Or is our childhood reaction to this whole enterprise the right reaction? Should we stop consuming animal products altogether?

What *are* we to think about the issue of consuming animals and animal products? It's all so perplexing.

The purpose of this book is to try to make this matter less perplexing.

We are going to defend a simple proposition:

If animals matter morally **at all***, we cannot consume them or products made from them and we are committed to a vegan diet, or a diet of vegetables, fruits, grains, beans, nuts, and seeds, and excluding all meat, fish, milk, cheese, other dairy products, and eggs.*

We are *not* going to present a general argument for animal rights.

We are *not* going to defend the notion that animals and humans have equal moral value.

We are going to focus on two principles that you and everyone else *already* accept and we hope to demonstrate that, based simply and solely on these two principles, we cannot justify consuming animal products. These principles commit us to a vegan diet.

These principles, which are widely shared moral intuitions and constitute our *conventional wisdom* about animal ethics, are as follows:

The first principle is that we have a moral obligation not to impose unnecessary suffering on animals.

No one doubts that.

We could, of course, have an interesting and lengthy

discussion about what "necessity" means and when suffering or harm is necessary. But determining what necessity means as an absolute matter isn't necessary for our purposes.

All that is necessary is that we all agree on what is *not* necessary: we all agree that it is not necessary to inflict suffering on animals for reasons of pleasure, amusement, or convenience.

So although we might disagree about whether particular instances of animal suffering are necessary, we would all agree that suffering imposed on animals solely because it brings us pleasure, or because we find it amusing or convenient, is not necessary.

The second principle is that although animals matter morally, humans matter more.

Some of us think that humans matter more because they are made in the image of God and have souls. Some of us may not believe in God at all, but still think that humans matter more generally or because they have certain abilities — they can write symphonies or poetry, paint pictures, or design buildings or bombs.

It really doesn't matter why most of us think that humans matter more and it doesn't matter whether that idea can be defended. We'll just assume that it's true.

A corollary of this second principle is that if there is a conflict that necessitates deciding between a human and a nonhuman, we must favor the interests of the human. For example, if we are on a lifeboat with another human and a dog, and we are confronted with some emergency that compels us to throw one overboard, the dog loses. The dog matters but the human matters more.

We would submit that there is virtually no one who would disagree with these two principles or doubt that they are widely shared moral intuitions. Yes, there are some people who have no moral concern for animals. But so what? There are some people who have no moral concern for other humans. Just as that fact does not negate our moral concern for other humans, the fact that some people have no moral concern for animals does not negate that most people do, and those who have no concern represent a minority. Nearly everyone regards animals as having *some* moral value and does not regard them merely as things.

So let's recap. We maintain that our conventional wisdom about animals is:

1. We have a moral obligation not to impose *unnecessary* suffering on animals; suffering imposed for mere pleasure, amusement, or convenience is, by definition, unnecessary.
2. Animals have some moral value but humans matter more than nonhumans; in a situation of conflict between a human and an animal, the animal loses.

We will not challenge these widely shared moral intuitions. We'll leave them in place and we'll show you that if you agree with them, they compel you to stop consuming animal products without even thinking about animal rights, much less embracing that notion.

In sum, we hope to persuade you that *what you already believe* commits you to a plants only — or vegan — diet.

Two Things Before We Begin

First, if you presently consume animal products, you may feel as though we're attacking you. We're not and we don't want you to feel as though we are.

Consuming animal products has been considered normal by most of us for all of our lives. We all have fond memories of family and friends at holidays and other special occasions, where there were always animal foods of various sorts served.

The purpose of this book is not to condemn you. It's not about judgment. Rather, it's about helping you to think clearly about something that you regard as a moral issue that has been nagging at you. To the extent that some of what we say may provoke or annoy you, we ask that you please try to get past your reaction to see whether you think that what we are saying makes sense.

Second, in order to keep this readable in terms of both style and length, we have avoided the sort of lengthy presentations that occur in traditional academic scholarship. We have also not included many footnotes. But factual assertions that would normally have citations are, for the most part, not controversial and can be easily verified.

I. We're All Michael Vick: Our Moral Schizophrenia

Remember Michael Vick?

Do you remember all the hoopla about football player Michael Vick, who was then quarterback for the Atlantic Falcons, and his involvement in a dogfighting operation on property he owned in Virginia?

Of course you do. It was covered by the media nonstop for weeks when it first came to light in 2007 and again when Vick came out of prison in 2009 and signed with the Philadelphia Eagles. He financed, participated in, and benefited from dogfights. He not only was involved in fighting dogs but he personally killed several dogs who did not perform to his satisfaction.

People weren't just upset; they were *furious* with Vick and many still are. There are football fanatics — Eagles fanatics — who now boycott the Eagles because of Vick. Vick keeps apologizing but people just won't forgive him. He still continues to appear in the news.

Why is our reaction to Vick so strong?

Is it because dogs have rights and we cannot make dogs suffer for any reason?

No, that's not it. We might not like the idea of any dog suffering but there may be circumstances in which we have a good reason to harm a dog. For example, if you are walking down the street minding your business and a dog attacks you, you may be in a situation in which you must harm the dog in self-defense. You might be in favor of using dogs in biomedical experiments if you thought that it might result in a cure for some disease.

The key to why we were and still are very angry with Vick is to focus on the words "good reason." Vick did a barbaric thing: he caused dogs to suffer and die, and the only reason he had was that he enjoyed it; he got pleasure from watching dogs fight and from his participation in that activity.

And *no one* would accept Vick's enjoyment of dogfighting as a good reason that would serve to justify what he did.

Why not?

Again, the answer is simple.

We all accept that it's wrong to inflict *unnecessary* suffering or harm on animals. We might disagree about whether necessity exists in any given situation. You might think that the possibility of obtaining some data from a painful biomedical experiment that uses a dog is justified; others (and we're included here) would disagree.

But the overwhelming number of us would agree that enjoyment or pleasure *cannot* constitute necessity or serve as a good reason for the infliction of suffering on the dogs.

Consider an example from the human context: if a person said that she believed that it was morally wrong to inflict unnecessary suffering on children but that beating children for pleasure was morally acceptable, we would understandably be confused. Putting aside whether we think it's ever a good idea to impose suffering on children, if enjoyment can suffice as a good reason to beat children, then there's no *bad* reason to beat children. *Every* reason is a *good* reason to beat children; *all* of the suffering imposed on children by beatings is, by definition, necessary. If pleasure or enjoyment can justify imposing suffering on children, then the principle that it's wrong to inflict unnecessary suffering on children would be meaningless.

The same analysis would apply if we talked about someone beating a dog rather than beating a child. No one would disagree that beating a dog for pleasure was morally wrong even if he or she believed that it was, for instance, acceptable to beat a dog who urinated on a carpet. And this is precisely why we all objected to what Michael Vick did; he did not have a good reason for what he did.

So the Vick matter implicates both of the moral intuitions that we discussed previously. Vick imposed suffering on animals and did not have a sufficient reason. And although we don't think dogs matter morally in the same way that humans matter — many of us would, for example, "sacrifice" a dog to find a cure for some illness — there was no conflict between humans and animals that required us to "sacrifice" the interests of the dogs. The only "conflict" Vick had involved his desire to use them for his pleasure, which was inconsistent with their well-being.

And that is not the sort of conflict that counts.

The suffering that Vick imposed was wholly unnecessary.

The Problem: We're All Michael Vick

The problem is that eating animals and animal products is, as a matter of moral analysis, no different from dogfighting.

We kill and eat more than 57 billion animals a year, not counting fish and other aquatic animals, which involves probably another trillion animals at the least. A billion is one thousand million. A trillion is one million million. So every year, we are responsible for a staggering number of deaths.

No one doubts that using animals for food results in significant suffering under the *best* of circumstances and, as a necessary matter, the killing of the animals. Although many of us think that the dairy and egg industries do not involve killing animals, that is, as we will see in more detail later, incorrect.

So let's apply the analysis that we all agreed was uncontroversial to using animals for food: have we got a good reason? Is there any necessity involved?

The short answer: no.

But wait! Don't we need to eat animals and animal products to be healthy?

No.

No one maintains that it's medically necessary to eat animal foods. Mainstream professional organizations, including the Academy of Nutrition and Dietetics, the American Diabetes Association, the American Heart Association, the British Dietetic Association, the British Nutritional Foundation, Dietician's Association of Australia, Dieticians of Canada, and the Heart and Stroke Foundation; research and teaching institutions, including the Mayo Clinic, UCLA Health Center , University of Pennsylvania School of Medicine, and the University of Pittsburgh School of Medicine; government agencies, such as the British National Health Service, the National Institutes of Health, and the Dietary Guidelines of the U.S. Department of Agriculture and U.S. Department of Health and Human Services; and even large managed care organizations, such as Kaiser Permanente, *all* acknowledge that a sound vegan diet is perfectly adequate for human health, and some of these groups claim that vegan diets may even have significant health benefits over diets containing animal products.[1]

And mainstream physicians are, with increasing frequency, pointing out that animal products are actually detrimental to human health.

We could now embark on a long discussion of the many studies that show that animal products are harming our health but we don't need to because whether or not you agree that consuming animal foods is detrimental, there is certainly no argument that animal foods are *necessary* for optimal health. That is, even if we do not believe that we will be *more* healthy if we eat a sensible vegan diet, we cannot reasonably believe we will be *less* healthy.

There is also broad consensus that animal agriculture is an ecological disaster. Although estimates vary, there is no question that animal foods represent an inefficient use of plant protein in that animals have to consume many pounds of grain or forage to produce one pound of meat. For example, according to Cornell University Professors David Pimentel and Marcia Pimentel,[2] it takes 13 kilograms (a kilogram is 2.2 pounds) of grain and 30 kilograms of forage to produce one kilogram of beef; 21 kilograms of grain and 30 kilograms of forage to produce a kilogram of lamb; 5.9 kilograms of grain to produce a kilogram of pork; 3.8 kilograms of grain to produce a kilogram of turkey; 2.3 kilograms of grain to produce a kilogram of chicken, and 11 kilograms of grain to produce one kilogram of eggs. Livestock in the United States consume 7 times as much grain as is consumed by the entire U.S. human population and the grains fed to livestock could feed 840 million humans who had a plant-based diet.

The Pimentel study states that one kilogram of animal protein requires about 100 times more water than does 1 kilogram of grain protein. According to another study,[3] one kilogram of beef requires 15,415 liters of water (a gallon is 3.78 liters); sheep meat (lamb and mutton) 10,412 liters; pork 5,988 liters; and chicken 4,325 liters. A kilogram of apples requires 822 liters of water; bananas 790 liters; cabbage 237 liters; tomatoes 214 liters; potatoes 287 liters; and rice 2,497 liters. Most estimates vary between 1,000 to 2,000 gallons of water to produce a gallon of milk.

The Food and Agriculture Organization of the United Nations states that animal agriculture contributes more greenhouse gases, which are linked directly to global warming, to the atmosphere than does burning fossil fuel for transportation.[4] According to the Worldwatch Institute, animal agriculture produces an estimated 51% of the worldwide total of greenhouse gas emissions from human activity. Moreover, a significant amount of fossil energy is required to yield an animal-based product. The average fossil energy input for all animal protein sources is 25 kcal of fossil energy input to 1 kcal of animal protein produced, which is more than 11 times greater than for grain protein production.[5]

Modern intensive animal agriculture techniques, known as "factory farming," have evolved to produce a large number of animals for market at a faster rate, at a lower cost, and by using far less land. This, of course, does not take into account the land that must be used to grow the grains and soy that is fed to these animals, so factory farming represents anything but an efficient use of land. An acre of land can provide food for many more people who consume a vegan diet than for those who consume animal products.

While these practices produce cheaper food, factory farms, or concentrated animal feeding operations (CAFOs), as the United States Environmental Protection Agency (EPA) refers to them, have serious environmental implications. For example, the United States Department of Agriculture reports that 1.37 billion tons of solid animal waste is produced annually in the United States (130 times greater than the human waste produced in the country). The excess quantities of nitrogen found in this manure can easily convert into nitrates, which, according to EPA, contaminate the drinking water of approximately 4.5 million people. When nitrates exist in the groundwater, they can be fatal to infants.[6]

The runoff into water and soil from factory farms is also responsible for the pollution of ground water and the widespread dissemination of hormones. Antibiotics are routinely added to the feed and water of poultry, cattle, and pigs to promote growth and prevent infection caused by unsanitary, intensive confinement; approximately 80% of the antibiotics that are produced are fed to animals used for food.[7] The use of antibiotics in animal agriculture and the resulting dissemination of antibiotics can contribute to antibiotic resistance in humans.

Animal agriculture is also responsible for water pollution, deforestation, soil erosion, and all sorts of unhappy environmental consequences. Again, you may dispute some of the details, but *no one* can credibly maintain that animal agriculture is not a net negative as far as the environment is concerned.

So, in the end, what's the best justification we have for imposing suffering and death on 57 billion land animals and at least a trillion aquatic animals, whom we do not need to consume for nutritional purposes, and given that this consumption results in ecological devastation?

Animal foods taste good.

We enjoy the taste of animal flesh and animal products.

We find eating animal foods to be convenient. *It's a habit.*

So how exactly is our consumption of animal products any different from Michael Vick's dogfighting?

The answer: it isn't.

We no more have a conflict with the animals we want to eat or whose products we want to eat, than Michael Vick had a conflict with the animals he wanted to use in fighting.

Vick liked sitting around a pit watching animals fight. The rest of us like sitting around a barbecue pit roasting the corpses of animals who have been treated as badly if not worse than Vick's dogs.

There is no difference between getting pleasure from dogfighting and the palate pleasure we get from eating animal products. In both cases, there is great suffering. In both cases, there is no necessity.

We're all Michael Vick.

Paying Someone Else to Do the Dirty Work

You may, at this point, be outraged and be thinking to yourself, or even saying out loud, "Of course there's a difference! Vick participated directly in the dogfighting and he enjoyed the suffering. I just buy animal products at the store." We certainly enjoy the results of animal suffering and death, but, unlike Vick, we don't enjoy the actual *process* of suffering and death.

Although that may be true, it is irrelevant from a moral point of view.

As any first-year law student will tell you, criminal law is clear in that it does not matter whether you pull the trigger or whether you hire someone else to pull the trigger. It's murder in both cases. It may be true that the person who pulls the trigger, plunges the knife, or swings the hatchet is a less "nice" person in some sense than the one who just pays the fee. After all, it takes a certain sort of person to engage in the physical act of killing another person. The person who actually does the act may be a sadist who enjoys watching other humans suffer. But it's still murder for both the person who does the act and sadistically enjoys doing so, and the person who pays for the homicide. We treat them the same legally because from a moral point of view, they *are* the same.

Similarly, the person who enjoys killing animals or watching them kill each other may be a more personally brutal person than the one who pays another to do the killing. So there may be a psychological difference between the person who pays another to kill and the person who kills, but as far as moral

17

culpability is concerned, there is *no* difference.

Would your assessment of Vick be any different if he financed the dogfighting operation but never attended it personally? It makes Vick a more brutal person that he actually enjoyed watching dogfighting and apparently participated directly in killing dogs, but that is a psychological matter and has no bearing on his moral culpability. There is no difference between person X, who kills the dog, and person Y, who says to X, "kill the dog but wait until I leave because I am squeamish."

The fact that we pay others to impose the suffering and death on animals does not get us off the moral hook.

There are some people who say that the difference between Vick and those who just consume animal products is that the latter do not really know the suffering that animal products entail.

We have a hard time accepting that position. After all, no one over the age of four thinks that meat grows on trees. Even if you don't know the exact process involved and don't know all of the horrible things that happen to animals, you know that animals have to be slaughtered to get meat and no one thinks that a slaughterhouse is anything but a place of horror.

Many of us have seen videos, photographs or even just written descriptions concerning the horrors involved in the production of meat, dairy, and eggs. And the response is often to turn away with a reply such as, "No, don't show me that; you'll put me off my dinner."

The bottom line is clear: we all know that our meat involves suffering and killing. No one doubts that. So it's not really even that those who consume animals don't know about the suffering. Of course they do. Yes, there is a psychological difference between Michael Vick and someone who just consumes animal products and would never kill an animal herself, but that is a psychological difference, not a moral one.

From all accounts, Vick treated his dogs in an appalling way. There is no doubt that many of them suffered a great deal. But frankly, the animals whose bodies many of us will eat tonight at dinner suffered every bit as much, if not a great deal more.

Similarly, many people who consume meat object to hunting. When we ask them why they object given that they eat meat, dairy, eggs, etc., they often reply, "Because there's something worse about killing the animal yourself. I would never be able to look at an animal and just shoot it with a bullet or an arrow."

Again, that response identifies a psychological fact; not anything that is morally relevant. Indeed, the animal who is raised and killed to make the hamburger probably had, on balance, a much worse life than the animal killed by the hunter. So, although killing the animal in both situations is not necessary, if there is any difference between these two situations, it is that the former is actually worse because it involves *more* suffering.

There is No Moral Distinction Between Meat and Other Animal Products

Some of you are probably thinking that you agree with us on the meat issue. You are, or lean toward being, a vegetarian. But, you ask, "What's wrong with dairy (milk, cheese, ice cream, yogurt, etc.) or eggs? They don't kill the animals for those products."

The short reply: that's a common misconception. But a misconception it is. Animals used for dairy and eggs do suffer, and they are all slaughtered just as those animals used only for meat are slaughtered. Most animals used for dairy and eggs are, like animals used exclusively for meat, kept in the intensive confinement and otherwise horrendous conditions of factory farms.

The nation's modern dairy industry utilizes primarily "dry-lot" dairies. These facilities are similar to beef feedlots, where cows used for meat are fattened, and dairy cows are kept standing or lying in their own manure in unsanitary holding pens. Contrary to popular belief, cows don't produce milk "automatically" and consider it a big favor that we milk them. They must be pregnant first. They are artificially and forcibly impregnated every year so that they are continually lactating. If we drink cows' milk, then the babies for whom it is intended aren't drinking it. Newborn calves are taken away from their mothers shortly — sometimes immediately and often after, at most, one or two days after birth — and no one seriously disputes that this causes distress to mother and baby alike.

Many of the female calves will become dairy cows (they are fed formula so that they don't take the milk); the rest of the females, and all the males, will become "meat" animals, with some being raised in confined (crate) conditions and slaughtered after about six months to be sold as veal. All cows, whether raised for meat or milk, will end up in the slaughterhouse. Dairy cows, who can live for 25 years, are usually slaughtered after four or five years when productivity starts to wane.

As a result of current dairy farming methods (diet, housing), dairy cows suffer from lameness, mastitis (a painful inflammation of the udder), reproductive problems, and severe viral and bacterial diarrhea. They are often given drugs to cause them to produce more milk. All dairy cattle end their lives in the same miserable slaughterhouses as do cattle used for meat, and many dairy cattle are too sick to walk to slaughter and are, therefore, dragged. Moreover, dairy cattle are mutilated; their horns are removed and tails are docked, or cut off, without pain management. Tail docking is a regular practice.

As for the egg industry, after hatching, the chicks are separated into males and females. Because male chicks will not be able to produce eggs and, because laying chickens are a specific laying breed that are not suitable to be "meat" animals, more than 100 million male chicks are killed in the United States alone every year by being thrown alive into grinding machines, suffocated in garbage bags, or gassed. Laying hens are confined in tiny battery cages where they get, on average, 67 square inches of space, or about the size of a single sheet of letter-sized paper, to live their entire lives. Most laying hens are subjected to forced molting, where the birds are starved for a period, causing them to lose their feathers and forcing their reproductive processes to rejuvenate, and to debeaking to stop

21

the birds from injuring each other. Those hens who are not confined in battery cages are raised in "cage-free" or "free-range" circumstances that still result in horrible suffering. And laying hens are all slaughtered once their egg-producing capacity decreases, usually after one or two laying cycles. So if all you eat are eggs, you are still directly responsible for the suffering and death of many chickens.

The bottom line: there is as much suffering in a glass of milk, or in an egg, as in a steak.

Remember Mary Bale?

Michael Vick-type examples abound.

Let's turn for a moment to Mary Bale from Coventry, in the United Kingdom, who dropped a cat into a dumpster where the unfortunate animal was trapped for approximately 15 hours before being released. Her callous act was captured on video and it was disseminated on the Internet.

The result was, as in the case of Vick, not merely anger; it was *outrage*.

Under a photograph the caption of which stated that Mary Bale "has faced vilification since being caught on CCTV camera putting a cat in a wheelie bin," one news report described the public reaction in this way:

> The "cat bin woman" from Coventry became reviled around the world, receiving abusive phone calls and death threats from as far afield as Australia, after what she described as a "split second of misjudgment" – which was captured on CCTV and uploaded to YouTube.
>
> Thousands of people signed Facebook pages claiming "Mary Bale is worse than Hitler" and calling for the "Death Penalty for Mary Bale" as she attracted newspaper headlines from "It's a Fur Cop" to "Miaow Could She?"[8]

Bale was prosecuted by the RSPCA for causing "unnecessary suffering" to an animal and was fined £250 but was also ordered to pay a victim surcharge and costs, a total of £1,436.04.

Think about this.

The public, most of which consumes animal products and thereby directly supports and participates in conduct that is in no way morally distinguishable from what Mary Bale did, condemned Mary Bale. And again, they didn't just get upset with her. They were, as in the Vick case, *outraged* at what she did.

Why?

For the same reason that people were upset with Vick. Bale inflicted suffering on the cat and it was simply not justifiable. She did it for no good reason.

The point is not whether what Mary Bale did was morally acceptable; it clearly wasn't. The point is that it is indistinguishable from what the rest of us do. Indeed, if it is distinguishable, it is because what we support and participate in every day is *worse* than what Bale did.

So the take away here is pretty clear: we condemn — in very strong terms — people like Vick and Bale for doing things that are indistinguishable from what the rest of us are doing.

Beyond Dogs and Cats

And our conventional wisdom does not apply just to dogs and cats. It applies to animals we use for entertainment as well as for food.

Think about bullfighting. Although there are people who enjoy this "sport" and support its continuation, most people think that it is repulsive and that it should be banned. When, in 2010, a bull impaled Spanish bullfighter Julio Aparicio through his throat and out his mouth, many people, and not just animal rights advocates, expressed the view that Aparicio got what he deserved.[9]

Why?

Bullfights are very violent events. A bull is tormented by inserting spears into his back muscles and he is eventually killed when a sword is thrust into his heart. And the only justification for this gruesome event is pleasure, in the form of entertainment.

Yes, some defenders claim that bullfighting is a form of art on par with painting, sculpture, dance, and music. But that is just another way of saying that it is a form of entertainment. There is no necessity, no need for this activity. There is no conflict between humans and animals that necessitates the suffering of the bulls.

We object to bullfighting because it violates conventional wisdom; it involves imposing unnecessary suffering on an animal.

But again, there is no difference between bullfighting and

using bulls and other animals for food. *Neither use is necessary.* Both uses serve only to satisfy the pleasure of humans. Indeed, the bulls and cows who end up in slaughterhouses have lives and deaths that are every bit as brutal as the life and death of a bull bred for fighting.

In fact, in most cases, the bulls killed in the arena are butchered and the meat is distributed to the poor. The difference between the two situations is that in one situation, the slaughter is not choreographed; in the other, it is.

And that is the *only* difference.

Ironically, when we do focus on food animals as individuals, particularly in situations in which they are suffering or in peril, we respond to them just as we would to a dog or cat.

We have all heard of situations in which animals other than "pet" animals are in peril and people go to great lengths to assist those animals. For example, not far from where we live, a cow fell into a pond and got stuck in the mud. Police and firefighters spent the following day, which was a holiday, trying to rescue the cow. They succeeded and went to extraordinary lengths not only to rescue the cow but also to keep her cool and comfortable during and after the rescue.

If these firefighters and police officers had not been involved in rescuing the cow that day, they would have most likely been attending a barbecue where cow corpses were being barbecued. But when confronted with a situation in which they saw the helpless cow, they responded just as they would respond if the helpless animal were a dog. If someone had seen the cow, and instead of helping her, had taken advantage of her inability to move and had tortured her in some horrible way, there is no doubt that we would have seen Vick-like rage from the public and a criminal prosecution for violating the anti-cruelty laws.

Think about how upset many people in Britain became when they learned that there was horse meat in their processed beef products. They were objecting to the fact that their meat had meat in it.

It's stunningly confused when you think about it.

* * *

So what inferences can we draw from what we've seen so far?

Most of us agree that although animals do not have the same moral value that humans do, they do have moral value, and that we have a moral obligation not to impose unnecessary suffering on them. Most of us agree that the imposition of suffering on animals for reasons of pleasure, amusement, or convenience does not constitute necessity. We look at people like Michael Vick and Mary Bale, or at practices like bullfighting, and we condemn them all because animals were made to suffer for no good reason.

The problem is that every time we consume animal products, we are participating in inflicting suffering on animals for no good reason. When it comes to animals, we are all Michael Vick. We are all Mary Bale. We all engage in conduct that is indistinguishable from bullfighting.

When it comes to animals, we suffer from *moral schizophrenia.*

Clinical schizophrenia involves delusional thinking. Our moral thinking about animals is literally delusional. We think of animals as having moral value; we think of ourselves as having an obligation not to impose unnecessary suffering on animals. We object to the imposition of suffering on animals when there is no compelling reason. We then proceed to impose horrible suffering on billions of animals without any reason that is more compelling than pleasure, amusement, or convenience.

27

At this point, we have only three options.

The first option is to decide that although we *say* that it's morally wrong to inflict suffering on animals without a sufficient justification, we don't really mean it. It's perfectly fine to inflict suffering on animals for any reason, including pleasure, amusement, or convenience. Our getting upset about Vick, Bale, and bullfighting is really nothing more than hypocrisy that we now acknowledge and accept.

The second option is that we have convinced you to stop consuming animal products or, at least, to resolve to do so. If that is the case, then you can stop reading now and just start searching for quick, easy, inexpensive, and healthful vegan recipes, of which there are many thousands readily available on the Internet.

The third option is that you are troubled and think that there is something to our argument but you are saying "But" and then thinking about *other* reasons that would cause you to retain the belief that animals really do matter but that it's acceptable for you to continue to consume them.

We examine those "Buts" in the following section.

II. "But...": The Excuses We Use and Why They Don't Work

Yes, you think that inflicting suffering on animals requires a good reason — some sort of necessity. No, pleasure isn't a good reason. Yes, you think that what Michael Vick did was terrible. No doubt.

But you say, "But..."

So in this section, we will explore the "Buts" that we use to try to distinguish our consumption of animal foods from dogfighting and other forms of animal "abuse." These "Buts" are the excuses that we use to pretend that what most of us do every day — without even giving it a second thought — is different from what Michael Vick did.

A preview: none of them works.

But... Where do you get your protein from?

This and similar "Buts," such as "But do you feel healthy without eating meat and dairy?", are part of our desperate but futile attempt to cling to the notion that we must continue to consume meat and other animal products or risk dying of malnutrition. That is, these "Buts" maintain that there really is some *necessity* involved in eating animals.

As mentioned earlier, mainstream medical authorities now recognize that a vegan diet is healthy. While adequate protein intake is one of the most commonly used reasons to counter a vegan diet, numerous studies and reports over the years across the United States, the United Kingdom, Canada, New Zealand, and Australia have confirmed that a vegan diet provides ample protein. Additionally, the United States Department of Agriculture (USDA) explicitly maintains that a vegan diet is capable of providing adequate amounts of protein.

Let us be clear and concise: *there is no credible evidence —* **none** *— that a vegan diet cannot supply the same quality of protein as that from animal sources.* The bottom line is clear: "Plant foods have plenty of protein."[10]

But... Will I get enough iron if I don't eat meat?

Yes.

We need iron for the formation of blood. Women need more iron than do men, and pre-menopausal women, especially pregnant women, need more than post-menopausal women. Iron is a central part of hemoglobin, which transports oxygen from the lungs to our tissues. It is also a constituent of certain enzymes. Iron is found in two forms: heme iron, which is about 40% of the iron found in meat, poultry, and fish, and non-heme iron, which makes up the other 60% of iron in animal tissue and all the iron in plant foods. Heme iron is more easily absorbed than non-heme iron and this leads some people to fear that a vegan diet will not have enough iron.

Have no fear.

Studies have shown that iron deficiency anemia is no more common among vegans than among the population generally. Many plant foods are actually higher in iron than animal foods. Spinach has 15.5 mg. of iron per 100 calories; steak has 0.9 mg. per 100 calories. Lentils have 2.9 mg per 100 calories; a pork chop has 0.4 mg per 100 calories. Whole grains, dried fruits, nuts, green leafy vegetables, seeds, and beans are also good plant sources of iron. Moreover, vegan diets tend to be higher in vitamin C, which increases the absorption of non-heme iron.

It is *easy* to obtain all the iron you need on a vegan diet, whether you are a man, woman (pre- or post-menopausal, or pregnant) or child. Indeed, it is easier to get all the iron you need from plant foods than from animal foods, and you'll certainly have to consume fewer calories of plant food to get the iron you need.

But... Will I get enough calcium if I don't consume milk and other dairy products?

Yes. In fact, if you don't consume dairy, and are conscientious about getting calcium from plant foods, you may well *reduce* your chances of getting osteoporosis.

"What?" you ask. "But we are told that we need milk and other dairy products in order to have strong bones." Yes, we are told that — by the dairy industry. But that does not mean that it is true. We don't need to drink the milk produced by another species; indeed, we are the only species that does so. In order to perpetuate the profitable notion that we need cow's milk, we are subjected to nutritional disinformation.

We need calcium for strong bones. The dairy industry tells us that cow's milk is the sole or primary source of calcium. But cow's milk is not the only, or the best source of calcium. Many plant foods are excellent sources of calcium: molasses, almonds, figs, sprouted sunflower seeds, sesame seeds, tofu processed with calcium sulfate, calcium-set tofu, bok choy, broccoli, Chinese cabbage, kale, mustard greens, okra, beans, and fortified soy, almond, coconut, hemp, and rice milks.

Moreover, not only is cow's milk not by any means the only source of calcium, it's not the best. The body needs magnesium to absorb calcium and cow's milk does not have sufficient magnesium to support its level of calcium. This results in the accumulation of excessive calcium in the body and that can lead to the development of calcium deposits in our joints and kidneys.

The consumption of animal protein, including the protein found in dairy products, causes our blood to acidify, which results in the leaching of calcium from our bones and our eventually excreting it from our bodies. So the consumption of dairy products not only does not prevent osteoporosis but it can actually cause it! In *The China Study*, Dr. T. Colin Campbell found that a protein found in cow's milk — casein — promoted cancer. Dr. Joel Fuhrman also notes in *Eat to Live* that there is a strong correlation between dairy lactose and heart disease.

Do vegans have to be sure to eat enough calcium-rich plant foods to ensure that they have sufficient calcium? Yes. But given that more than 60% of Americans who consume milk are deficient in calcium, diligence is not only a matter for vegans. Indeed, given the other issues involved with cow's milk and the proteins contained in it, the vegan, once again, has the nutritional advantage.

But... Will my children get enough iodine?

The BBC reported about a study apparently showing that women who had too little iodine while pregnant had children with lower IQs and reading scores. The solution? "Academics advise women of child-bearing age to maintain iodine in their diets by eating dairy products and fish. Women were warned not to take seaweed pills, as they contain too much iodine." [11]

First of all, seaweed pills *may* have too much iodine. Many do not. Second, eating small amounts of seaweed can provide all the iodine we need. Other plant sources of iodine include baked potatoes and navy beans. Fortified (or iodized) salt also supplies iodine.

Breastfeeding women need 250 micrograms of iodine per day; other adults need 150 micrograms. Plant foods can supply this amount.

But... I heard about someone who became ill after eating no animal foods.

And what about all of the people you know who ate animal products and have developed cancer, heart disease, etc.?

This "But" is yet another attempt to characterize consuming animal products not as a matter of pleasure but one of physical necessity. As we mentioned earlier, even traditionally conservative organizations, including professional and government bodies, and managed care organizations, agree that an "appropriately planned" vegan diet can be completely healthy. And there is *no* evidence to the contrary.

It is, of course, possible to get ill eating only plants just as it's possible (and more likely, actually) to get ill eating animal products. Although some vitamin B-12 is made by bacteria in the human body, not enough is reliably made for our needs and the unhealthy habits that humans have prevent maximum production and absorption of the endogenous B-12. Therefore, it is necessary to supplement B-12 from external sources whether you consume a vegan diet *or* a diet of animal foods. So *all* humans need to get their B-12 from somewhere outside their bodies. We get our vitamin B-12 from yeast; omnivores get theirs from meat. But *all* B-12 comes from bacteria — whether it is found in the gut of ruminating animals who get it from fermenting plant material in their hindgut, or in certain strains of nutritional yeast. So if you adopt a vegan diet but don't consume an alternative source of B-12, such as yeast, yes, you *may* get ill. But there are plenty of people who have B-12 deficiencies despite their consumption of animal foods.

How about DHA and EPA, the long-chain fatty acids that aren't found in plant foods and that people eat fish to get? Most people can convert the short-chain fatty acids found in chia seeds, walnuts, dark leafy greens, and canola oil into long-chain fatty acids. Or you can get long-chain DHA and EPA directly from the source that fish get it — algae. There are now many DHA/EPA supplements that are algae derived.

Occasionally, one hears about a parent prosecuted for manslaughter because their child died on a "vegan" diet. But when the facts are revealed, we learn that the parents had fed the child only iceberg lettuce (or something similar) and nothing else for some extended period of time.

If the parents fed the child nothing but steak three times a day for an extended period, the child would also become ill. But no one would say that the child died or became ill from eating meat. They would say that the parents engaged in abuse by feeding the child an inadequate diet. The same is true of a diet consisting only of lettuce. That's not a vegan diet; it's a ridiculously inadequate diet.

In the 30 years that we have been vegans, we have heard of a number of people who supposedly became ill while on a vegan diet. An inadequate vegan diet will make you ill because it is inadequate and not because it is plant-based. Eat nothing but celery and soy yogurt and you will not feel very energetic. Surprise, surprise.

We have also encountered people who say that their bodies "tell them" that they must eat meat or fish or chicken or dairy or whatever. But such assertions are really no different from saying, "I like the taste of meat (or whatever)." In other words, they are assertions about palate pleasure and nothing more. A related issue is the "need" to eat meat or other animal products based on blood type. The so-called "blood type diet" has been debunked as junk science.

But… Doesn't God want us to eat animals?

A frequently raised "But," particularly in the United States, is that God wants us to eat animals, or that God placed animals on earth for us to eat.

The most usual form of this "But" is that *Genesis*, the first book of the Old Testament, which is common to both the Jewish and Christian traditions, says that God created the world and gave dominion and control over the animals to humans.

Doesn't that tell us that God wants us to eat animal products?

Wait just a minute; it's a bit more complicated than that.

The first thing to do is to go and read *Genesis*. It simply does not say what everyone who uses this "But" seems to think.

In *Genesis*, we are told that God created the world and gave "dominion" over it to humans but — and here's the surprise — *no one was eating anyone in the beginning*. God told humans "I have given you every herb bearing seed, which is upon the face of all the earth, and every tree, in the which is the fruit of a tree yielding seed; to you it shall be for meat."[12] And then God told all the animals and birds, "I have given every green herb for meat: and it was so."[13]

So in the beginning, before Adam and Eve disobeyed God by eating the fruit of the forbidden tree and were driven from the Garden of Eden, everyone — humans and animals alike — ate *only* plant foods. It was only after God destroyed the world with a flood that he told Noah that humans are allowed to eat "[e]very moving thing that liveth."[14]

We started off in harmony with God as beings who consumed plants. When we fell out with God and were driven from Eden, God *permitted* us to kill animals as an accommodation to our imperfect state. The Old Testament at least suggests that we should be moving in the direction of getting back to the ideal state.

When the prophet Isaiah talks about the coming of the Messiah and the re-establishment of God's kingdom on earth, how does he describe it? First of all, there will be peace between humans, who will "beat their swords into ploughshares, and their spears into pruninghooks: nation shall not lift up sword against nation, neither shall they learn war any more."[15] But peace will also extend to and amongst nonhumans: "The wolf and the lamb shall feed together, and the lion shall eat straw like the bullock: and dust shall be the serpent's meat. They shall not hurt nor destroy in all my holy mountain, saith the Lord." [16]

But we are not biblical scholars and we don't want to overstate the case here. We think that using the Old Testament to make a slam dunk case for not eating animal foods would be unsound. But it would also be unsound to say that the Old Testament provides slam dunk support for the view that God is giving us a green light to kill and eat anything we want because we like the taste, or because it would be easier to stop in and pick up a bucket of fried chicken than prepare some rice and beans or one of the many other vegan recipes that can be prepared very easily and quickly.

The Old Testament, like almost all religious scriptures, is ambiguous at best and contains contradictions. Indeed, the entire problem with using documents like the Old Testament as support for *anything* is that the Old Testament can be read to support *everything*, including all sorts of things that we would all acknowledge as terrible, such as human slavery, murder, and rape.

Consider the story of Lot, which is also in *Genesis*. Two angels came to his home and Lot receives them as his guests. The men of Sodom came to Lot's house and, thinking that the angels were human men, asked Lot to produce his guests so that the men of Sodom could, well, sodomize them. Lot responded that the townsmen could not have his guests but that they could take his two virgin daughters instead, and do with them as the men saw fit.[17] And Lot is one of the good guys of the Old Testament!

The Bible prohibits all sorts of things, such as rounding off the side-growth of your heads (sideburns) or cutting the edges of beards,[18] tattoos,[19] wearing blended fabrics of linen and wool,[20] contact with a woman who is menstruating,[21] women speaking in church,[22] and men whose testicles or penis are not intact from attending church.[23] If two men are fighting and a wife of one of the men should try to help her husband by grabbing the testicles or penis of the man beating her husband, her hand is to be cut off.[24] And the death penalty is prescribed not only for killing another but also for other offenses, such as cursing your parents.[25]

The bottom line is that even the most fundamentalist person does not follow the scripture of her or his religion to the precise letter. So it's clear that these texts cannot be relied upon exclusively to resolve every particular moral problem.

It would seem that the most that one could argue is that humans matter more because they are made in God's image and have souls, or have "special" souls. Such a view is, of course, just an aspect of conventional wisdom. That is, most people think that animals matter morally but that humans matter more than animals. Religious people may believe that humans matter more because God created animals as spiritual inferiors. But many people who are not religious and, indeed, who may be atheist, think that humans matter more because they are cognitively more sophisticated.

Even if you believe that you have a soul and animals don't, and that we ought to prefer the interests of a human in any situation in which we must choose — that is, in any situation of legitimate conflict — that gets us right back to the fact that when you are deciding what to eat tonight, there is no conflict. There is only a choice. If you choose the animal product, you are participating in suffering and death in the absence of any sort of conflict or compulsion. Your only justification is that you enjoy consuming animal products or that it is more convenient for you to do so.

Think about it this way: imagine that Michael Vick were to say that dogfighting was okay because dogs don't have souls. Would you buy that? Imagine that Vick says God wants us to fight dogs because they don't have souls. Would you buy that?

You would respond to Vick that God's creating us in God's image means that in situations of conflict between human and nonhumans, we ought to protect the human interest over the animal interest. So in the situation in which a person is in a *true* emergency situation, such as when she is starving to death with no plant foods to eat, it would make sense for a religious person to say that God wants her to kill and eat an animal and that she ought to do so.

But saying that God wants us to eat animal foods when we are *not* in that sort of emergency situation is no different from saying that God wants us to fight dogs. If you would find the latter to be objectionable — outrageous, perhaps — you should find the former so as well.

But... Isn't eating animal products "natural"?

This "But" is like saying that God wants us to eat animals but we don't need to bother with God. Something else that is big and important — nature — wants us to eat animals. If we don't eat animals, we are acting against nature. We are behaving in an *unnatural* way. That's powerful stuff — even if you're an atheist. In fact, "But Natural" is like "But God" without God. It seeks to establish necessity, but without God.

But why do we think that nature intends, whatever that means, that we eat animals? The usual response is to say that we are physically adapted to eat meat and other animal products.

Putting aside that many people are lactose intolerant, and that many physicians are pointing out that animal products are detrimental to human health, the *most* we can say is that we *can* eat animal products. There is nothing about our bodies that suggests that they are designed to do so.

Humans compare physically much more to herbivores than to carnivores. Carnivores have well-developed claws. We don't have claws. We also lack the sharp front teeth carnivorous animals need. Although we still have canine teeth, they are not sharp and cannot be used in the way carnivorous animals use their sharp canine teeth. We have flat molar teeth, as seen in herbivores, such as sheep, that we use for grinding.

Carnivores have a short intestinal tract so that they can quickly expel decaying meat. Herbivores have a much longer intestinal tract as do humans. Herbivores and humans have weak stomach acid relative to carnivores who have strong hydrochloric acid in their stomachs to digest meat.

Herbivorous animals have well-developed salivary glands for pre-digesting fruits and grains, and have alkaline saliva that is needed to pre-digest grains, as do humans. Carnivorous animals do not have similar salivary glands and have acid saliva.

We are told by advocates of the Paleolithic diet that we should eat the way our "ancestors" ate. But how did they eat? As biologist Rob Dunn wrote in Scientific American, "[F]or most of the last twenty million years of the evolution of our bodies, through most of the big changes, we were eating fruit, nuts, leaves and the occasional bit of insect, frog, bird or mouse. While some of us might do well with milk, some might do better than others with starch and some might do better or worse with alcohol, we all have the basic machinery to get fruity or nutty without trouble."[26]

And, as we stated earlier, the evidence is quite clear that we don't need animal products to be optimally healthy. You would think that if we were intended to eat animal products, those of us who don't (and haven't for decades) would suffer deleterious health effects. But we don't. We do just fine. We have to make sure we get vitamin B-12, which humans do not manufacture, or at least not in reliable quantities. But all humans have to get B-12 from somewhere. Carnivores get it from meat; vegans get it from nutritional yeast, other fortified food, or supplements. But all B-12 comes from microorganisms.

As we also stated earlier, humans also need fatty acids that they don't manufacture. Most people get their essential fatty acids from eating fish. The fish get it from consuming algae. We get these fatty acids directly from an algae supplement. We also eat flaxseeds and walnuts, which provide these nutrients.

So while there is considerable evidence that animal foods are detrimental to human health, we don't want to get into a battle of studies here to convince you that it's healthier not to eat animal products. We do, however, want to make clear that the very best a consumer of animal products can say is that her diet is no better than that of someone who eats a balanced diet of non-animal foods.

In sum, there is no evidence that nature requires that we eat animal products. Indeed, the extant evidence is to the contrary.

But... What if everyone ate just plant foods? There would not be enough land to grow food!

This "But" maintains that if we all ate just plant foods, there would not be enough room to grow all the necessary crops. Therefore, eating meat and other animal products is, contrary to what has been said, necessary. This distinguishes eating animals from dogfighting.

This "But" is not only wrong; it is *very* wrong.

According to the EPA, approximately 80 percent of all corn grown in the U.S. is consumed by livestock, poultry and fish and "[o]ver 30 million tons of soybean meal is consumed as livestock feed in a year."[27] Moreover, according to the U.S. Department of Commerce, "[w]hile 56 million acres of U.S. land are producing hay for livestock, only 4 million acres are producing vegetables for human consumption."[28]

These statistics clearly illustrate how we are using our planet's resources — including land, water, and energy — inefficiently by consuming meat and other animal products. Nonetheless, meat and dairy production continues to be on the rise across the globe. The demand across the United States and Europe is so high that it cannot be met within national borders. These meat industries have taken to Latin America to meet this demand, and at least 20 percent of the Amazon's forests have already been converted into pastures and feed crops. These practices inefficiently and cheaply feed the United States and Europe, while taking away the efficient and natural agriculture of these developing nations.

Opponents of plant-based agriculture argue that the expansion of crop production would result in the complete destruction of arable land because the soil depletion will become so severe that the land will be incapable of maintaining our current methods of monoculture, or repeatedly harvesting the same crop. However, this argument completely ignores the effects of today's practices. In the United States, livestock account for more than half of soil erosion.

Researchers in the United Kingdom have noted that the arable land in the United Kingdom is incapable of providing adequate amounts of some meat substitute crops, such as soy, lentils, and chickpeas. But they also noted that the cultivation of different pulses, such as various other dry beans and peas, would eliminate such concerns.

Regardless of whether or not feasible crop alternatives would exist for the United Kingdom, this would not be a new concern faced by European countries. Currently, the continent as a whole has the arable land capacity to feed its entire population with plant protein, but it does not have even close to the land capacity to feed all of its farm animals. The European Union found that only 20 percent of what Europe's farm animals eat comes from the continent, while the remainder must be imported. Because most of these imports use up the land in developing countries, this animal-based method of feeding Europe contributes directly to the depletion of the resources of developing nations, thus contributing to their continued impoverishment.

What it essentially boils down to is that our production of food, regardless of what it is, has a large ecological impact. As our population continues to grow, if we persist in eating the amount of animal products we do, that impact will continue to take an exponentially larger toll on our planet than would the production of only plant foods.

And what about the field mice, snakes, birds, and other creatures who are killed when crops are planted and harvested? Would we kill *more* animals if we had a vegan diet than if we ate animals and animal products?

The answer is clearly: no. It takes more land to grow plants that we feed to animals we eat than it would take if we consumed the plants directly. And the production of meat has the largest impact on the destruction of the world's biodiversity due to its role in pollution, deforestation, soil erosion, land degradation, greenhouse gas emissions, and so on.

There are some people who argue that even if we have fewer acres under cultivation, whatever crops we eat will result in more animal deaths because more wild animals are killed in crop production than in raising animals on pastures. But this position ignores that the land used for crop production can provide up to 10 times the amount of protein than can be produced from animals raised on pastures. So *even if* more wild animals are killed in crop production than in raising animals on pasture, the number of wild animals killed *per consumer* in crop production will be a fraction of the number of animals killed in raising animals on pasture because one acre of crops can produce protein for so many more people than one acre of pasture used to raise animals.

But... What if I were on a desert island starving to death?

The short answer to the question posed by this "But" is that you aren't. Nor are you stranded in the middle of the ocean adrift on a lifeboat with another human and a cow and someone has to be thrown overboard. Nor are you passing by a burning house that holds two occupants, a human and an animal, only one of whom you have the time to save.

This "But," and similar ones, seek to identify a situation in which consuming animals might be necessary but which you are *not* in, and then generalize to situations in which you *are*, where there is no necessity to consume animal products. It doesn't work.

For some reason, many of us seem to want to formulate general moral principles on desert islands, lifeboats, and while standing in front of burning houses. These are notoriously bad places to try to devise moral rules because they usually require that we choose amongst several morally unsatisfactory choices in a situation of emergency. We then seek to generalize that choice to cover situations in which the emergency that limited the choices does not exist.

But let's go to the desert island. There you are, starving to death and there is neither a coconut nor carrot available. There are, however, rabbits (although we are not sure what they are eating if there's no vegetation on the island). Is it morally acceptable to kill and eat a rabbit in such circumstances?

Let's assume that it is.

So what? What does that tell those of us who aren't starving to death on a desert island about whether it is morally acceptable to eat a steak tonight?

It tells us *nothing*. In the first situation, there is a conflict; in the second, there is not. Our moral intuitions tell us that *in a situation of true conflict*, humans prevail. So eating the rabbit on the desert island is morally acceptable according to that intuition. But that intuition has *nothing* to do with situations in which there is no conflict.

Let's think about the situation in a human context. You are stranded on the desert island with John and Mary. You are all starving but John is also ill and will die soon. You and Mary kill and eat John.

Yes, it's a disgusting thought but things like this have happened. It's still murder and it's still a crime but it is often punished less severely because we understand that, as a moral matter, killing and eating John in such a circumstance is different from garden-variety murder. Eating John in such circumstances, although wrong, would at least be understandable and would not merit the sort of moral condemnation evoked by other acts of unprovoked homicide. After all, if you are starving, you don't really have a choice and moral condemnation requires that you were able to choose differently but did not and chose to do the wrong thing.

Similarly, in the example involving the rabbit, I have a choice of starving to death or killing the rabbit. That's not really a good choice. In fact, it's not really a choice at all.

So why should we apply the analysis that would make sense in a situation in which there is *no* choice to a situation in which there *is* choice? We would not say that, even if an act of cannibalism in an extreme situation of isolation and starvation is morally excusable, eating another human is fine whenever you feel hungry and choose to eat another human because that is what you prefer. What is morally tolerable in the situation in which there is no choice is not necessarily tolerable in the situation in which there is choice. Similarly, the fact that we would say that it is morally acceptable to eat a rabbit in a similar extreme circumstance does not mean that it is acceptable to do so when there is choice.

Now assume that you have been rescued from the desert island. You are now walking down the street and you pass by a burning house containing a human and a dog. Our moral intuition tells us that in situations of real conflict, humans win and animals lose. We promised not to upset our moral intuitions and we're making good on that promise. So whom do you save? You save the human. After this terrific act of heroism, you head home to eat dinner. What does your choice of saving the human tell you about the morality of eating chicken for dinner?

Nothing. Absolutely *nothing.* Our moral intuitions may tell us that in situations of genuine conflict between humans and animals, humans win. But our intuitions also tell us that in situations in which there is no conflict, we cannot inflict suffering on animals simply because we get enjoyment from doing so.

Again, to see this clearly, all we need to do is consider what we would think if the burning house contained two humans. You don't know either human but one is a great deal older than the other and your moral intuitions tell you that you ought to save the younger person simply because she is younger. Would you conclude from this that it would be acceptable morally to torture older people, start farming them or start using them in biomedical research?

Of course not. Your moral intuitions might lead you to save the younger person precisely because you could only choose one to save and, in that unhappy situation, you chose to save the younger person. But that choice leaves completely unaffected your other intuition that hurting someone — anyone — requires a moral justification.

There is a tendency to use these desert island / lifeboat / burning house scenarios to demonstrate that — because our moral intuition is that animals have moral value but less moral value than humans do, and because we would choose the human over the animal in a genuine conflict situation — animals have *no* moral value and we can inflict suffering on them even when there is no conflict.

But that simply does not follow, and it explains why many of us feel deeply uneasy about continuing to consume animal products in the absence of any necessity. Even if we think that animals have less moral value than humans do, the point of this book is that if they have *any* moral value whatsoever, we cannot justify imposing *any* suffering on them just because we get enjoyment from it. Similarly, just because we would choose one human over another in an emergency situation, that does not mean we would support the view that it is acceptable to subject some humans to any suffering just because we enjoy it.

If animals matter morally at all, if they are not just things, imposing *any* suffering on them because we enjoy it or the results of it cannot be morally acceptable. So the fact that you would eat the rabbit on the desert island, or throw the cow out of the lifeboat, does not in any way affect the moral principle that imposing unnecessary suffering is morally wrong and suffering for the sake of palate pleasure is, by definition, unnecessary.

A variation on this "But" involves people who live in places where they don't have a choice of what to eat. There are a few examples of indigenous people in remote parts of Canada, or on the African continent (Kenya), who consume a diet of meat where there are few or no non-animal foods. The idea is that such situations are similar to the desert island scenario where one can choose to eat animals or die.

We don't need to get into a factual inquiry about people in Canada or in Africa and whether they really have no choice and must eat animal foods or perish. The position we are arguing for here is that in any situation in which there is really no choice, animal use could be considered morally acceptable under the conventional rule that we should not impose unnecessary suffering. In situations in which there really is no choice, there is a sort of necessity that removes the conduct from the proscription of the general moral rule.

But our guess is that just as there is no one reading this who is stranded on a desert island, or adrift in a lifeboat, there is no one reading this who lives somewhere where he or she really has no ability to get non-animal foods.

The point remains: for anyone who *does* have a choice — and that includes just about everyone reading this right now — a choice to impose suffering in the absence of necessity violates what we claim to be the moral principle that we all accept.

But... What would happen to all of those animals if we did not eat them?

This is an easy one: if we stop consuming animal foods, we would stop bringing domesticated animals into existence.

Period.

What would we do with the animals we have here now? Well, that depends on what you think are our moral obligations to those animals. It is not an option to just release these animals into the wild. The cows, pigs, chickens, turkeys, etc. that we see today are not wild animals. They were domesticated by us to be food animals.

If you regard animals as having greater moral value than conventional wisdom allows, you may think that we should take care of the animals who are here now until they die a natural death and just not bring more into existence. Alternatively, you may think that we should just eat the animals and animal products we have now but stop bringing any more animals into existence.

The ultimate answer is, however, the same under either (or any) scenario: if we think that we should stop consuming animals, we should stop bringing domesticated animals into existence.

There are three responsive "Buts."

But... What about natural diversity?

A responsive "But" is to point out that if we did not have domesticated animals, we would somehow lose a piece of natural diversity. It's as if having a vegan world would be one big violation of the Endangered Species Act.

It is, on at least two levels, beyond absurd to use the word "natural" in any context that involves domesticated animals.

First, animals have been so manipulated genetically that many do not even resemble the animals we had 100 years ago. Cows have enormous udders; pigs and turkeys develop such massive body weight that they cannot walk. Domesticated animals are anything but natural in any sense.

Second, domesticated animals, whether a long while back or now, are just that: they're beings who have been domesticated. They are not part of the "natural" world. They are part of the world that *we* have created. They are beings we caused to be developed and produced for our purposes.

The "natural" world will be much more "natural" without domesticated animals. There is no "extinction" when it comes to domesticated animals.

But... What about their right to live?

Another responsive "But" is that by eliminating domestication, we actually make animals worse off than if they lived and died in unpleasant circumstances.

This response assumes that it is better for an animal to have even an unpleasant life and death than never to have lived at all. So by having a vegan diet, we harm animals generally because they would not exist if we were all vegans. We are doing animals some sort of *favor* by consuming them. Indeed, we would be *harming* animals if we didn't consume them.

In addition to requiring that we make a completely speculative and ultimately baseless guess about whether animals would, if they could, choose not to live at all rather than live a horrible life and suffer a horrible death, this position completely negates our intuition that animals matter morally and that we ought not to make them suffer unless it is necessary to do so. This position says, in effect, using animals for food is unnecessary and results in a great deal of pain, suffering, and death but it is better to have that unnecessary suffering and death than not to have it. So if we adopt this position, we, in effect, discard our moral intuition that animals matter and that causing them suffering for frivolous reasons is immoral.

To put the problem another way: if this works for the animals we eat, it works for Michael Vick's dogs. Sure, they suffered and many died. Sure, dogfighting is a completely frivolous use of animals. But Vick's dogs were better off living and suffering than not living at all and so dogfighting is just fine. Indeed, this position would allow us to engage in a wide range of animal torture on the view that a life with some torture — even a significant amount of torture — is better than no life at all. Do we really need to explain what horrendous results come from this way of thinking?

So, in addition to any other problems that this position has, we cannot maintain it at the same time we maintain that we need a good reason to inflict suffering and death on animals and that pleasure, amusement, or convenience cannot suffice as a good reason. If we take this position, we, in effect, endorse the notion that animals are just things that we can use, make suffer, and kill just because we enjoy doing so.

But... What about their right to reproduce?

A third responsive "But" is that if we don't have any more domesticated animals, we will violate the rights of animals to reproduce.

This "But," in essence, seeks to make the point that if we don't continue to eat animals, we are somehow going to violate their rights, thus providing an extraordinary example of how desperate we get when we want to justify eating animal foods.

Putting aside that, for the majority of domesticated animals, sex and procreation are unpleasant and frightening experiences, it is nothing short of bizarre for people who don't believe in animal rights and who consume meat and other animal products to be concerned about the right of animals to reproduce.

But... We brought food animals into existence to be eaten; that is what they are here for.

And?

First of all, if this is relevant, what is wrong with dogfighting? After all, *all* domesticated animals, whether dogs, cats, cows, sheep, pigs, chickens, turkeys, or even farm-raised fish were brought into existence by us. So if this justifies our eating animals, it justifies our using animals for dogfighting, bullfighting, and everything else.

That is, to accept this "But" is, in effect, to say that animals do not matter morally at all; that they are just things and that we *don't* need a good reason to inflict suffering on any domesticated animal. To accept this is to say that we don't accept the conventional morality we claim to accept.

Second, if we do have moral obligations to animals but our having some responsibility in bringing them into existence lets us off the moral hook, then where does that leave our children? They would not exist but for us. Does that mean we can justify harming them for pleasure, amusement, or convenience?

But... Animals used for food don't suffer as much as dogs used in fighting.

This "But" seeks to distinguish the Michael Vick situation from our eating animals by suggesting that animals used for food suffer less than dogs used to fight.

As a factual matter, animals used for food are, under the most "humane" circumstances, treated horribly; they are literally *tortured*. Do they suffer less than did Michael Vick's dogs? Animals used for food, whether for meat, dairy, or eggs, are, as a matter of routine industry practice, subjected to pain, suffering, and distress throughout their lives. And their deaths in slaughterhouses are always terribly frightening and horribly violent. Therefore, it's probably the case that animals used for food suffer *more* than dogs used for fighting.

But that's not the point.

The point is that our conventional wisdom would say that *any* suffering can't be justified without a good reason — some necessity — and pleasure can't suffice as an acceptable justification. The issue is not whether dogs used for fighting suffer more than cows, chickens, turkeys, pigs, fish, or other animals used for food. They *all* suffer and they all suffer significantly. We are not talking about "suffering" a light slap. That is clear. Animal agriculture, particularly on the scale required to feed billions of people, necessarily results in horrible suffering under the most "humane" conditions.

And, as we have discussed, there is no justification for eating animals any more than there is a justification for fighting dogs. Both behaviors serve one primary interest: our pleasure. There is nothing necessary about either use of animals.

So even if, as a general matter, animals used for food suffered less than dogs used for fighting, what would that mean? *Nothing*.

Our conventional wisdom is that we cannot justify inflicting any level of suffering on animals without a good reason and pleasure is not a good reason. To say that animals used for food suffer a great deal but may suffer less than dogs used in fighting does not address the fact that animals used for food suffer a great deal under the very best circumstances and most "humane" conditions. If we determined that Michael Vick's fighting dogs suffered less than the animals we eat, would any of us think that dogfighting is morally alright? *No.*

We should also say that we reject the notion that we can say with any confidence who suffers more in any particular circumstance. Do cows suffer more than fish? We don't even know what that question means when we are talking about individuals from the *same* species. If two humans were afflicted with an illness, what would it mean to ask whether one was suffering more than the other? Would any of us find that question meaningful? We can't even make meaningful assessments about physical pain or suffering, or emotional distress, where members of our own species are involved.

Trying to ask this question when it comes to different species makes an impossible situation even more impossible. We may be able to recognize cow suffering more because cows, like us, are mammals. We can more easily understand suffering in a mammal than we can, say, in a bird or a fish. However, that does not mean that the bird or the fish suffers *less*. It means that the bird or the fish suffers *differently*. But again, that is irrelevant. The idea behind the notion that we ought not to subject animals to unnecessary suffering is not that only suffering like ours is relevant. The point is to acknowledge a moral rule that animals are not things, that they have some moral value, and that we have to justify harming them.

And to say that one animal is harmed less than another animal does not mean that it is acceptable to harm the former. Yes, it is worse to impose 10 units of suffering than 5 units of suffering. But we have to justify *both*. Indeed, we have to justify imposing even *one* unit of suffering. And we agree that pleasure cannot be a sufficient justification for imposing pain and suffering on animals. There must be a compulsion, a necessity.

But... Do animals feel pain in the same way that humans do?

Maybe yes; maybe no. But it doesn't matter whether they do or don't.

The only issue is whether they can feel pain; any being who can feel pain has an interest — a preference or desire — not to feel pain. It does not matter whether an animal feels pain in the same way that a human does or even in the same way that other members of the same species feel pain.

Part of our conventional wisdom is that nonhuman animals, like us, feel pain and that we all have an interest in not suffering pain. Although there are some people who will say things like, "Animals don't feel pain," or "Animals don't have feelings," no one really believes that. After all, we have had laws requiring that we treat animals "humanely" for hundreds of years now. Those laws may be pretty ineffective but we have them on the books because we all recognize that animals feel pain, that they can suffer, and that they have feelings. After all, we don't have laws requiring the "humane" treatment of rocks or trees.

There are, however, people who will say that although animals feel pain, they don't feel it in the same way that humans do. So what? We don't know whether humans all feel pain in the same way. You may not feel pain in the same way that your friend feels pain but you both have an interest in not experiencing pain irrespective of how each of you experiences that pain. And that's what matters: that you are capable of having an experience that you don't want to have. It does not matter whether another human experiences pain differently from the way that you do. What matters is that she, too, is capable of having an experience that she does not want to have. You and she are similar — however differently you experience pain — in that you can both experience something that neither of you wants to experience. You have the same interest even if the experience itself is different.

The same is true of animals. Indeed, humans and all of the animals we routinely exploit for food, with the *possible* exception of mollusks such as clams and oysters, are all *sentient*. That is, they have subjective perceptual awareness; they have the capacity for feeling or sensation. Humans and nonhumans are all similar in this respect: they are all capable of experiencing pain; they are all beings who have an interest in not experiencing pain. That interest is the same even if the experiences are themselves different.

We should add that there is a tendency to think that humans suffer more because they are more sophisticated intellectually. Maybe yes; maybe no. It may well be the case that animals suffer more because of cognitive differences with humans. A visit to the dentist, although painful, may present a great deal less suffering and distress than a dog's visit to the veterinarian. The human knows that the pain will end shortly and understands the reason why the pain is being inflicted; the dog does not, and this may make the dog's suffering worse.

Finally, consider that when we object to what Michael Vick did, we don't do so because we think that the dogs felt pain in the exact same way that humans do. We know that dogs feel pain and our moral outrage about what Vick did is not contingent on our thinking that dogs and humans experience pain in the same way. All that matters is *that* dogs can feel pain, not *how* they feel pain. Our conventional wisdom says that such pain cannot be morally justified unless we have a good reason to inflict that pain. Our moral obligation is not linked to a similarity of experience; it is only linked to a similarity of interest. And all sentient beings have the same interest in not wanting to experience pain and suffering, however different that experience may be. And the obligation not to impose pain and suffering without a good reason is not in any way linked to the actual experience of a particular being; it is a moral obligation to respect an interest that all sentient beings have.

But... Do fish really feel pain?

Yes.

Many people who engage in fishing think that fish do not feel pain. But scientists have proven that view wrong.[29] There are receptor sites in the heads of fish that respond to damaging stimuli and fish show reactions to harmful substances.

How about clams, oysters, mussels, and scallops? Are these mollusks able to feel pain? It's not clear whether they can or not. We err in favor of not eating them because the evidence is not conclusive one way or the other. But other mollusks, such as the squid and octopus, are among the most neurologically advanced of all invertebrates, and they are clearly sentient. Lobsters and snails are also sentient.

Remember, the issue is not whether fish or mollusks feel pain in the same way that humans feel pain. The only issue is whether they can feel pain; any being who can feel pain has an interest — a preference or desire — not to feel pain. It is that interest we regard as morally significant when we say that we need a good reason to ignore that interest and impose that pain.

But... Aren't there laws that require the "humane" treatment of animals?

Yes, there are laws that supposedly require that we treat animals "humanely" and that we not inflict "unnecessary" suffering on them. They exist in every state in the United States; they exist at the federal level; and just about every country in the world has some law requiring "humane" treatment.

Despite any differences, all of these laws share one feature in common: they are *useless.*

First, these laws do not prohibit *uses* that are unnecessary; they supposedly prohibit only *treatment* that is not necessary to achieve a given use. We have seen that eating animals and animal products is not necessary for human health. Therefore, *all* of the suffering incidental to using animals as food is unnecessary! It *all* runs afoul of what we claim to embrace as an uncontroversial moral principle: that animals matter morally and that we need some justification for imposing suffering and death on them — and that the pleasure of taste can't suffice as a justification for consuming animal products just as the pleasure of watching dogs fight can't justify what Michael Vick did.

So if we think that the existence of laws requiring "humane" treatment is even relevant, we have misunderstood the issue. Even if these laws were effective, which, as we will explain below, they are not, there would still be a great deal of animal suffering under the very best scenario. And a situation of less *unnecessary* suffering is still in conflict with the notion that we claim to accept that we can only justify *necessary* suffering. And necessary suffering requires some conflict, some compulsion. Our palate pleasure fails on that score just as Vick's amusement at watching dogfights failed.

This point cannot be emphasized enough because so many people, when confronted with the argument that we cannot justify eating animals or animal products, react almost spontaneously with this "But." What they fail to see is that the moment we start talking about a law that prohibits imposing "unnecessary" suffering in the context of an activity that is itself not necessary, we are talking nonsense. A rule prohibiting "unnecessary" suffering or requiring "humane" treatment in the context of dogfighting would make no sense because *all* of the suffering incidental to dogfighting is unnecessary. So to talk about the "humane" treatment of animals we eat or use to produce meat, dairy, eggs, or other animal products is to talk about reducing suffering, but where *none* of the suffering is necessary, such an approach entirely misses the point!

Let's consider an example from the human context. Assume you have a rule that prohibits the "unnecessary" suffering of rape victims and requires their "humane" treatment. Now if person X decides he is going to rape person Y, it is always better if he harms Y less than more. It is better if X does not beat Y in addition to committing the rape. But if someone proposed a law that prohibited the infliction of "unnecessary" suffering on rape victims and required their "humane" treatment, we would all agree that made no sense and was morally offensive. Sure, it is always better to do something morally wrong in a less harmful way than in a more harmful way. But that does not mean that doing something immoral in a less harmful way makes the immoral act moral.

Second, given the economic realities of the world, the notion of "humane" treatment is — like the idea of Santa Claus or the Tooth Fairy — comforting in some sense at least to the consumer, but a complete fantasy.

Animals are *property*. They are *economic commodities*; they have a *market value*. We may sentimentally value the dogs, cats, and other animals who live in our home. But as far as the law is concerned, they are just our property. We can take them to a shelter or to a veterinarian's office, where they can be killed, whenever we want.

Animal property is, of course, different from the other property that we own in that animals, unlike cars, computers, machinery, or other commodities, are sentient and have interests. All sentient beings have interests in not suffering pain or other deprivations and in satisfying those interests that are particular to their species.

But it costs money to protect animal interests. As a general matter, we spend money to protect animal interests only when it is justified as an economic matter — only when humans derive an economic benefit from doing so. That is, the law generally prohibits imposing suffering on animals only when we get an economic benefit from doing so.

Consider the Humane Slaughter Act in the United States, enacted originally in 1958, which requires that large animals slaughtered for food be stunned and not conscious when they are shackled, hoisted, and taken to the killing floor. This law protects the interests that animals have at the moment of slaughter, but does so only because it is economically beneficial to do so. Large animals who are conscious and hanging upside down and thrashing as they are slaughtered will cause injuries to slaughterhouse workers and will incur expensive carcass damage. Therefore, stunning, or rendering large animals immobile, makes good economic sense. To do so will reduce injury to workers and carcass damage that results in lower market prices. Of course, these animals have many other interests throughout their lives, not just including an interest in avoiding suffering at the moment of slaughter, but these interests are not protected because it is not economically efficient to do so.

Interestingly, the Humane Slaughter Act does not apply to chickens, who are slaughtered by the billions annually and comprise about 95% of the animals we slaughter. Why not? Because in 1958, it was not thought that covering chickens under the Act would provide any economic benefit. Many animal advocates are arguing that poultry should be covered under the Act and their argument is based, in part, on the notion that the supposedly "humane" way of killing chickens, which involves gassing them before they are decapitated and defeathered, is economically efficient and will reduce production costs. Employees are often injured during the present slaughtering process and, because the chickens struggle before they die, there is a fair amount of carcass damage.

Animal welfare laws generally either explicitly exempt what are considered the "normal" or "customary" practices of institutionalized animal use, and, in particular, exempt the animals we raise and kill for food, or courts interpret pain and suffering imposed pursuant to those practices as "necessary" and "humane." That is, the law defers to industry to set the standard of "humane" care. This deference is based on the assumption that those who produce animal products — from the breeders to the farmers to the slaughterhouse operators — will not impose more harm on animals than is required to produce the particular product, just as the rational owner of a car would not take a hammer to her car and dent it for no reason. In any event, the effect of most animal welfare laws is to make the production process more efficient.

Beyond the economics of production efficiency, animal welfare laws that require "humane" treatment are really not about animals; they're about humans and making humans feel better about using animals. We can comfort ourselves with the idea that we are acting in a "humane" way.

Let's be clear: the laws requiring "humane" treatment allow for the *torture* — and we are using that term literally and deliberately — of the animals we raise and kill for meat and other animal products. Most of the meat, dairy, and eggs we eat are produced from animals kept in intensive confinement on the factory farms that we discussed earlier. And factory farms are nothing but large torture chambers.

But... What if we improved the treatment of animals we use for food?

Let's assume that we all agree that animals used for food have horrible lives and horrible deaths, and the laws requiring "humane" treatment are, for the most part, useless. But what if we changed all that, went from factory farms to Old MacDonald's farm, and abolished intensive confinement in favor of better conditions? Couldn't we do that?

That is exactly what some animal advocates propose. In fact, most of the large animal organizations in the United States, Britain, and elsewhere campaign for larger cages for egg-laying hens, more space for nursing pigs and veal calves, and for slaughterhouses that are more "humane." Many of these animal organizations endorse and promote various labeling schemes that inform consumers that they are supposedly buying a "higher welfare" product.

There are two relevant considerations.

First, like the previous "But" concerning "humane" treatment laws, this "But" misses the point. Even if the reforms proposed by animal advocates would significantly improve animal welfare, which, as we explain below, is not the case, what that would mean is that animal suffering would be reduced. But as the use of animals for food is not necessary at all, it would still not make our consumption of animal foods consistent with the moral principle that we claim to accept: that imposing any suffering and death on animals requires some necessity, some compulsion.

If we reformed dogfighting to be less violent, there may be a reduction of the suffering of the dogs but no one who thinks that what Michael Vick did was wrong would change her mind and support dogfighting. Dogfighting is wrong because, as a practice, it results in unnecessary suffering and death. Consuming animal foods is wrong because, as a practice, it results in unnecessary suffering and death. Making either practice more "humane" does not result in either practice conforming to our moral intuitions on the need to justify animal suffering. The fact that animal advocates are joining with industry to support and praise "happy" meat, eggs, and dairy does not mean that the consumption of those products is morally acceptable any more than a religious person declaring the perpetration of an act of violence to be the will of God makes it morally right to kill.

Second, the reforms being proposed by animal organizations hardly mean the abolition of factory farming or a return to the 19th-century family farm. On the contrary, most of what animal organizations are proposing involves reforms that increase production efficiency or involve, at most, only tiny increases in production costs that won't have any significant market effect. For example, gassing chickens (rather than just decapitating them) reduces carcass damage and worker injuries; increasing space for pigs and veal calves results in less-stressed animals who have lower veterinary bills. These reforms are *very* modest. They are to animal ethics what padded, as opposed to unpadded, waterboards for use at Guantanamo Bay are to human rights.

The *most* "humanely" raised animals are still kept and killed in horrible circumstances. Period. All of this talk about "happy" animal products is about *us*; it's about making us feel more comfortable about doing something that nags at us. It's about keeping us from having to recognize that we are all Michael Vick so that we continue to consume animal products. It's really got *nothing* to do with the animals. They continue to suffer horribly irrespective of what "happy" label — "free-range," "cage-free," "organic," "Certified Humane Raised and Handled," or "Freedom Food" — is slapped on their corpses or the products we make from them. And it's even worse when large animal organizations praise and support these "happy" products.

As we discussed above, it costs money to protect animal interests. Sure, it's possible *in theory* that we might all be willing to pay a great deal more for animal products and that standards could improve in significant ways. But that's just theory. Very few people could afford animal products that were produced in a way that provided significantly more protection to animal interests.

And let's be perfectly clear: even if we *completely* eliminated every vestige of factory farming, *which is an economic impossibility*, and went back to a system of what we think of as the idyllic family farm, there would still be a great deal of animal suffering. The storybook image of farming is a fantasy, designed to make children comfortable with eating creatures who look just like the stuffed animals that they love.

Moreover, anyone who would care enough to pay the significantly higher cost of such production would probably care enough so as not to eat animal products at all. Additionally, given economic realities and free-trade rules, even if welfare standards were raised significantly in one place, demand for lower-priced, lower-welfare products would force the higher-welfare producers out of business except, perhaps, to serve a very small and affluent niche market.

But... What if we treated food animals just as we treat our pets?

This is a variant on the "But what if we improved the treatment of animals we use for food?" It recognizes that we cannot treat animals "humanely" as long as we are engaged in factory farming or even smaller farming. And it therefore asks the following: if we had a cow or a couple of chickens, raised them in our backyards, treated them just as we do our dogs, cats, or other animal companions whom we regard as members of our family, and slaughtered them painlessly, what would be wrong with eating them or products made from them?

There are four replies here.

First, as a practical matter, it would be largely impossible to raise and slaughter animals without some considerable pain and suffering being involved even under the most ideal circumstance. That gets us back to the idea that less suffering is certainly better than more suffering but that, if we regard animals as having moral value, we need to be able to justify *any* pain and suffering that we impose.

Second, as a psychological matter, this suggestion is most unrealistic. We would not eat animals if we thought of them in the way that we think about our dogs, cats, and other companion animals.

We knew a couple who decided that they wanted to

continue to eat animal products but that they were going to produce their meat, milk, and eggs themselves on a small farm that they had. They triumphantly declared that they could raise and kill animals without making them suffer any more than did their dogs and cats, whom they loved and whose interests they always sought to protect.

We were skeptical precisely because we knew that once they treated cows, pigs, and chickens with the same sort of attitude that characterized their treatment of their dogs and cats, they would be unable to eat those animals just as they would not eat their dogs and cats. And that is precisely what happened.

After about two years, they gave up the farm and stopped eating all animal products. "They became family; we just couldn't eat them," was how they put it. For those of us who live with animal companions, the thought of eating them never crosses our mind. If we started relating to food animals in the way in which we related to our nonhuman companions, we would not eat them either.

That's the point. If the light goes on and we see that we are all Michael Vick, the thing to do is to stop being Michael Vick and stop consuming animal products. The solution is not to restructure things to treat animals we are going to eat as we treat dogs and cats.

Third, as a philosophical matter, this question assumes that if we *were* able to use animals without making them suffer, our painlessly killing an animal does not, in itself, amount to harming the animal.

This is in marked contrast to how we think about humans. Yes, suffering is bad, but we view death, even a painless one, as a bad thing. We humans have an interest in continuing to live. Death frustrates that interest, which is separate from an interest in not suffering. We don't want to suffer; we also don't want to die. Animals, many say, don't want to suffer but they don't care about dying unless the act of killing involves suffering; it is the suffering that is a problem for the animal, not the killing.

This idea, in one form or another, has been around for hundreds of years. The moral intuition that we now all accept that animals matter morally, but less than humans, and that we can use animals when it is necessary to do so as long as we minimize suffering, was an idea that emerged in the 19th century. It assumed that it was acceptable to use animals when necessary because, unlike humans, they are not self-aware and have no interest in continuing to live; that is, they do not prefer, or desire, or want to remain alive.

That idea, which most certainly makes us feel better about killing animals for food, was crazy in the 19th century. It is crazy now.

To say that any sentient being is not harmed by death is most peculiar. Sentience is not a characteristic that has evolved to serve as an end in itself. Rather, it is a trait that allows beings to identify situations that are harmful and that threaten survival. *Sentience is a means to the end of continued existence.* Sentient beings, by virtue of their being sentient, have an interest in remaining alive; that is, they prefer, want, or desire to remain alive.

To say that a sentient being is not harmed by death denies that the being has the very interest that sentience serves to perpetuate. It would be analogous to saying that a being with eyes does not have an interest in continuing to see or is not harmed by being made blind. The Jains of India expressed it well long ago, "All beings are fond of life, like pleasure, hate pain, shun destruction, like life, long to live. To all life is dear."[30]

The notion that animals are not self-aware is based on nothing more than a stipulation that the only way to be self-aware is to have the self-awareness of a normal adult human. That is certainly *one* way to be self-aware. It's not the only way. As biologist Donald Griffin, one of the most important cognitive ethologists of the twentieth century, noted in his book, *Animal Minds*: if animals are conscious of anything, "the animal's own body and its own actions must fall within the scope of its perceptual consciousness." We nevertheless deny animals self-awareness because we maintain that they cannot "think such thoughts as 'It is *I* who am running, or climbing this tree, or chasing that moth.'" Griffin maintains that "when an animal consciously perceives the running, climbing, or moth-chasing of another animal, it must also be aware of who is doing these things. And if the animal is perceptually conscious of its own body, it is difficult to rule out similar recognition that it, itself, is doing the running, climbing, or chasing." He concludes that "[i]f animals are capable of perceptual awareness, denying them some level of self-awareness would seem to be an arbitrary and unjustified restriction."[31]

It would seem that *any* sentient being must be self-aware in that to be sentient means to be the sort of being who recognizes that it is that being, and not some other, who is aware. When a sentient being is in pain or distress, that being necessarily recognizes that it is she or he, and not some other, who is in pain or distress. There is some*one* who is conscious of being in pain and who has a preference not to have that experience.

Even if animals live in some sort of "eternal present," which we doubt to be the case, that still does not mean that they are not self-aware, that they have no interest in continued existence, or that death does not harm them. It just means that their self-awareness is different. Animals would still have a sense of themselves *in each particular moment*. They would still want to get to the next moment of the present. Their sense of self-awareness may be different from that of a normal adult human, but it would not be accurate to say that they are not self-aware or that they are indifferent to death.

We see this where humans are involved. If a human is mentally disabled and is not self-aware in the same way that a normal human is, we do not think that such a human is without an interest in life or that death is not a harm to her or him. She or he may be self-aware in a different way than others but is still self-aware in a morally relevant way so that we would regard treating her or him exclusively as a resource — which is how we treat nonhuman animals used for food — as morally wrong.

In sum, if a being is sentient — that is, if she is perceptually aware — then she has an interest in continuing to live and death harms her. It is not necessary to have the autobiographical sense of self that we associate with normal adult humans in order to be self-aware. And a humanlike sense of self-awareness is not necessary to have an interest in continuing to live.

Fourth, let's get back to practicality. Even if everything we just said were completely wrong and it were possible to have animal agriculture with the animals being treated like dogs and cats, not suffering at all, and being allowed to die of old age, the reality is that products made from such animals are simply not available *now* in the world in which we live. So what difference does it make to your choice about what to eat tonight?

The answer is clear: *none*.

There are some people who, when they find out we don't consume milk (or anything from anyone who had eyes or a mother), will tell us a story about their great grandparents' cow who was treated as a member of the family.

Although we do not accept as an empirical matter that the cow in the family farm situation did not suffer, our usual follow up is not to argue that point but to ask what happened to the baby cows who were born as the result of having this cow be pregnant regularly so she would continue to produce milk. The reason we ask that question is that we know the answer: the males were sold as veal calves as were some of the females. The rest of the females became dairy cows. This undercuts the argument that there is no suffering in the family farm situation in a way that most people can understand.

But there is always the person who comes back with, "All of the babies were allowed to live on the farm and were never sent to slaughter. I am telling you, these cows never suffered." Again, there are many things that could be said in response to this wildly fantastical characterization but among the most efficient timewise is to ask, "Do you have any access to milk made in that way now?

The answer is always, "No."

Our reply is always, "So even if that were all true, what relevance does it have to your decision now to consume milk?"

The response is always either an acknowledgment that the hypothetical situation is meaningless in terms of our actual moral behavior or a remark expressing irritation — indicative of the fact that we have asked a question that cannot be answered in a satisfactory way.

A related responsive "But" we get at this point is, "But... What if I rescued and adopted a chicken and treated her as I would my dog or cat. Would it be alright to eat her eggs?" Putting aside that such a system could not supply eggs to many people (unless we all adopted chickens), the reality is that because chickens have been bred to lay such an unnatural number of eggs, their bodies are depleted of nutrients and the chickens will often and usually eat their own eggs once they realize that they are not fertilized. And hens often become very distressed when their eggs are taken. So in the very best case scenario, which certainly could not supply any quantity of eggs as a commercial matter, we end up taking eggs that the hens need for themselves and putting them in situations in which they suffer distress. And unless we are going to keep them until they die of natural causes, which can be 10 years or more after egg production wanes, we will end up killing them.

The bottom line is clear: there is no way to produce animal products — whether meat, dairy, or eggs — without suffering under the best of circumstances, and death. It just can't be done. And if it is not necessary for us to consume animal products, then we cannot justify even a greatly reduced level of suffering, and more "humane" death on the non-existent Old MacDonald's Farm — just as we agree that a more "humane" dogfighting operation would not make Michael Vick's conduct justifiable.

But... Don't we have to solve human rights issues first?

This is a frequently heard "But." We explain the reasons why we cannot justify consuming animal products and someone asks, "Yes but what about the problem of battered women?"

This is no different from discussing the issue of the inadequate response of the legal system to the problem of battered women, only to have someone respond, "But what about the problem of pedophilia?" There is always something else that could be addressed!

And we note that when we ask people who ask this question what *they* are doing to address human rights issues that they claim are more important than the issue of animal exploitation on which we are working, nine times out of ten, the answer is usually that they aren't doing anything.

But in the event that you are one of those people who really is concerned about and devoting time, money, or energy to human rights problems, we want to explore this "But" further.

There is, of course, implicit in this question the notion that humans matter more in a moral sense than do animals and so we should be focusing on human problems and not animal problems. As we stated at the outset, we aren't going to challenge the conventional wisdom that although animals matter morally, humans matter more. Yet this "But" still goes nowhere.

First, no one is asking that anyone stop working on or being concerned about human rights issues. On the contrary, we agree that there is a terrible amount of racism, sexism, heterosexism, ableism, classism, and all sorts of other injustice, and we think it's great that people care about and work on these issues.

But what does that have to do with what we are talking about in this book, which is simply that if you agree animals matter at all, you are committed to not consume them any longer?

The answer: *nothing*.

Even if you think that any and all human rights issues are more important than the issue of animal exploitation, you have to eat while you are fighting for those great causes. How does eating, for example, tofu instead of steak impede your ability to fight for human rights causes? It doesn't. If anything, a healthy vegan diet will give you more energy to pursue those causes.

And that's where this analysis comes in.

So you leave your morning meeting with the local child protection agency in connection with your efforts to get better protection for kids and you want to grab something for lunch. Where is the conflict between you and the cow that justifies your having a hamburger? Indeed, if you have the burger, then you have just, by your action, rejected the principle that you claim to accept: that inflicting suffering on animals requires a moral justification.

You don't have one.

Second, even if you are only concerned about human rights issues, you ought to be concerned about animal exploitation as well because it is directly connected to a significant human rights issue. As we discussed earlier, the amount of resources required to produce animal foods is multiples of what is required to produce plant foods. Although there are certainly political issues that hamper the distribution of food, it is also the case that animal agriculture and a diet of animal foods is increasingly a threat to world hunger, our water supply, our topsoil, etc.

But... What about Hitler? He was a vegetarian.

No, he wasn't.

But let's not worry about something as insignificant as historical facts being wrong. Let's assume that Hitler consumed no animal products. What would that say about not consuming animal foods?

Absolutely nothing.

The thinking behind the "But Hitler" point is that Hitler cared about animals and that led him to undervalue humans and, as a consequence, do terrible things to them. Therefore, if you care about animals, you'll undervalue humans and do terrible things to them. So keep consuming animal products. Take the kids to chow down a bucket of fried chicken tonight; you don't want them to become Nazis.

Putting aside the patent absurdity of such a position, remember that Joseph Stalin killed millions of people, as did Chairman Mao. Both ate animal products. Cambodia's Pol Pot, Japan's Hirohito, Belgium's King Leopold II, and Spain's Francisco Franco were also responsible for horrible atrocities. They all consumed animal foods. So to the extent that you think that what you consume will incline you towards being a mass killer, you'd be better advised not to consume animal foods given the correlation between being a mass killer of humans and being a consumer of animal foods.

There is a sense in which the "But Hitler" point is intended to set up an unfavorable association: Hitler had a characteristic — he was a vegetarian (which he wasn't) — and Hitler was an evil man so we should reject any characteristic associated with him. But Hitler also took baths. So we should not bathe because we don't want to be like Hitler. He also wore clothes and drank water. If you don't want to be like Hitler, stop wearing clothes and drinking water.

You get the idea.

But... What about plants?

The scene: we are at a dinner party. We are minding our business eating our vegan meal. Someone asks why we are not eating the meat and dairy products that others are eating. They ask if it is about health. We say, "No, it's about ethics." And then we hear almost immediately, "But what about plants?"

This "But" is often fitted to the particular plant food we happen to be eating; for example, "But what about that broccoli you're eating? Wasn't it in pain when it was cooked?"

Next to "But Hitler," this "But" is the silliest of all "Buts."

No one really thinks that plants are the same as animals. If someone ate your tomato and your dog, no one would regard those as similar acts.

Let's be clear here: there is *no* scientific evidence that plants think or exhibit any sort of mental activity so that we can say that plants have interests. There is *no* scientific evidence that plants have any sort of mind that prefers, or desires, or wants anything. There is *no* scientific evidence that dropping broccoli into boiling water is in any relevant way similar to slaughtering a cow or pig or chicken, or dropping a live lobster into boiling water.

We could present a discussion about botany here but it's really not necessary as no one *really* maintains that plants are sentient and can experience pain, or that they have perceptual awareness of anything. The concern about plants got its start in

1973 when a journalist and a writer who focused on alternative science wrote *The Secret Life of Plants* based on the discredited experiments of, among others, Cleve Backster. Backster was originally an interrogation specialist for the Central Intelligence Agency and, in 1968, published a paper in the *International Journal of Parapsychology* claiming that plants had thoughts and emotions, and could read human minds.

But wait. In his 2012 book, *What a Plant Knows: A Field Guide to the Senses*, Tel Aviv University scientist Daniel Chamovitz reports that plants can see, smell, think, and feel. He's a recognized scientist and he seems to say we're wrong, right?

Wrong. *Scientific American* interviewed Chamovitz and asked him point blank, "Would you say, then, that plants 'think'?" Chamovitz replied, "No, I wouldn't." He added, "Just as a plant can't suffer subjective pain in the absence of a brain, I also don't think that it thinks."[32]

Chamovitz and people, like philosopher Michael Marder, who, in his 2013 book, *Plant-Thinking: A Philosophy of Vegetal Life*, defends "plant ethics," point to instances in which plants react to stimuli. No one doubts that they do. They are alive. They conduct various activities, some of which are very complex, at the cellular level. But they conduct *nothing* at a cognitive or conscious level because they lack consciousness and cognition altogether.

Plants *react*; they don't *respond*.

Will a plant turn toward the sun? Sure. Will it do so even if by turning in that direction the plant will be mowed down? Sure. Will any animal behave in that way? No. Animals *respond*; plants *react*.

A bell will react if you run electricity through the wire to which it's attached. Does that mean the bell is responding? No. Does that mean that the bell is conscious? Sentient? No, of course not. Bells react; plants react. Neither is conscious; neither is sentient; neither responds to anything. They are not the sorts of things that can respond; they are only the sorts of things that can react. Indeed, they are *things*.

A dead giveaway here is that those who defend "plant ethics," when confronted with the indisputable fact that plants are not sentient, start making claims that although plants are not sentient, they are, to use an expression that Marder used in a debate we had with him sponsored by Columbia University Press, capable of "nonconscious intentionality."[33]

"Nonconscious intentionality." What in the world does that mean? How can one intend to do something in a nonconscious way? Isn't consciousness necessary for intention? Do plants engage in activities that achieve certain states of affairs? Yes. But it begs the question to talk about "intentionality" in this context. At this very moment, there are all sorts of biological processes going on in our bodies. We hope that these processes are conducted toward certain ends, such as cellular repair, and not toward other ends, such as tumor formation. But can we talk about the "intentionality" of cancer cells? Only if we beg the question and assume that cellular reactions have a cognitive component. We could say that the electrically charged particles that travel down the wire are nonconsciously intending to make the bell sound. That would be silly but no more silly than saying that a Venus flytrap nonconsciously intends to close its "jaws" on a fly.

Advocates of "plant ethics" often argue that we simply cannot say whether plants are sentient. They may be sentient in a way that we cannot yet recognize. We just don't know. For example, although Chamovitz acknowledges that plants can't think, he adds, "but maybe that's where I'm still limited in my own thinking!" There are three simple responses here.

First, you could say the same thing about anything. You could, for instance, claim that we cannot really know whether a particular blade of grass is Einstein reincarnated. It may very well be Einstein; we just do not have the tools yet to recognize that it is. Making absurd claims and saying that they may not be absurd because it's possible that they may not be absurd is an absurd endeavor.

Second, unless you want to ignore the principle of evolution, you would need to explain *why* plants would evolve a characteristic that would be entirely useless to them. If plants could feel pain, there is nothing that they could do about it except to suffer that pain. Plants can't run away.

Third, even if, contrary to everything we know, plants were sentient, we still kill more plants when we eat animals than when we consume those plants directly. So when someone who is eating a one-pound steak asks you about the plants you are eating, you can remind him or her that the cow from whom the steak was taken was once a sentient mammal who had a nervous system very similar to our own and who was unquestionably sentient. In order to produce that one-pound steak, about 16 pounds of plant protein were needed. So we have a sentient mammal who died, along with 16 pounds of supposedly sentient plants.

So even if plants were sentient, the person eating the steak and the person eating the plant foods directly are engaged in different acts, and the former's act is a lot worse. But then, if the person eating the steak really had a moral concern about plants, or about the suffering of sentient beings generally, she or he would be consuming the plants directly.

Although the concern about the sentience of plants is silly, this "But," like "But Hitler," is an indication that the person you're talking with recognizes that there is something wrong, or at least questionable, about eating animal foods. Just as no one *really* thinks that Hitler's dietary regime is relevant to anything, no one *really* thinks that your broccoli suffered when it was cut or boiled. And, like "But Hitler," "But Plants" is a "But" that, despite its silliness, is often used by otherwise intelligent people. In any event, the fact that someone is offering a "But," particularly a very silly "But" like this, may be a strong indication that she or he is provoked and troubled about eating animal foods.

But... Eating animal products is a tradition.

There is one word that, whenever you hear it in the context of an argument in favor of some position, you know with certainty that the person using the word to defend the position has nothing substantive to say. That word is *tradition*.

To use tradition or culture to justify anything is just another way of saying that we've done something for a long time, so we are justified in continuing to do it. In other words, it offers not one single bit of support for the practice being challenged.

We *know* that people have been eating animal foods for a long time. That's the point. We're challenging that behavior as being inconsistent with our conventional wisdom that we must be able to justify imposing suffering or death on animals. So repeating the fact that people have been eating animal foods for a long time is completely useless as far as moving things along is concerned. It merely re-states the problem under discussion and does not provide any sort of resolution to it.

Virtually anything worth talking about from a moral point of view has been going on for a long time and is part of *someone's* tradition.

Take female genital mutilation, for example.

This absolutely horrible practice involves the partial or total removal of external female genitalia, for the purpose of ensuring pre-marital virginity and inhibiting extra-marital sexual conduct. Although one may very well object to male circumcision, female genital mutilation is a great deal more severe and, in addition to reducing or eliminating any pleasure that a woman gets as a result of sexual intercourse, there are considerable risks and side effects, including fatal hemorrhaging, cysts, infections, chronic pain, and a whole range of gynecological and obstetrical complications. The age range for this mutilation is from several days after birth to age 15 or 16. It is sometimes done later.

There is a great deal of opposition to this practice and a number of international bodies, including the United Nations, have sought to end it. The argument is pretty straightforward: doing something like this to anyone raises serious human rights issues; doing it to babies, young girls, and teenagers, who cannot provide any informed consent, is monstrous.

Despite efforts that have been going on for years now, this practice persists.

Why? What is the possible justification?

Putting aside the completely silly reasons related to invalid concerns that a woman with her genitalia intact cannot safely handle food or that a woman's clitoris is dangerous to a man's penis or a baby's head, the primary reason is simple: it's a tradition. It's part of the culture in places in Africa, the Near and Middle East, and Southeast Asia. They've been doing it for a long time. Female genital mutilation goes back to ancient Egypt.

So what can we infer from this?

We can infer that something horrible has been going on for a long time.

We cannot, however, infer that the practice is morally acceptable because it has been going on for a long time.

The same non-argument is used to defend bullfighting. If you criticize bullfighting in places such as Spain, those who defend it will shout at you about the fact that this is an honored tradition. Again, what does that mean?

It means that people have been torturing bulls for fun for a long time.

So what?

There is one sense in which we must be sensitive about tradition arguments. They are often made *to* people in societies that have been exploited or oppressed *by* those who exploited or oppressed them. So some defenders of female genital mutilation will bristle when people from the United States or Western Europe, which do not have a great track record when it comes to Africa, criticize Africans for this practice. Or indigenous people who live in northern Canada will bristle when non-indigenous Canadians or those from the United States criticize their killing of seals or whales.

We should, of course, be sensitive to these concerns and to the effects of other unjustifiable practices, such as colonization. But that does not mean that people get a free pass to do other morally unjustifiable practices. Two wrongs don't make a right.

Finally, the use of tradition to justify eating animals is particularly absurd. *Everyone*, including people from *every* ethnic group, can claim that animal foods are part of their cultural tradition. One of the reasons that "But Tradition" resonates in other contexts is that it is usually made to defend a practice that a fairly small number of people regard as sacrosanct, such as female genital mutilation or bullfighting.

But when we use tradition to justify something like the consumption of animal foods, which everyone does, it is like using tradition to justify sexism, or racism, or something else that everyone does. In this instance, the use of tradition is particularly absurd and amounts to nothing more than saying that the practice is a longstanding one. There is no valid claim that eating animals, as an activity, is something that is part of the identity of the particular group in any special way.

Yes, people may claim that their particular ethnic animal foods are part of their group identity, but that is like saying that a particular sort of pornography is part of the identity of a group that practices sexism. When we are talking about pervasive, ubiquitous behaviors, such as consuming animal foods or sexism, using tradition is nothing more than saying that something being criticized has been going on for a long time. And, instead of regretting that something morally wrong has been going on for far too long, the tradition argument says, "We've done it for a long time so we can do it some more."

But... We're at the top of the food chain.

What food chain?

This "But" is another way of asking whether our power and ability to exploit animals makes it morally right to do so. We would immediately see the problem if this "But" were raised in a context involving humans. For example, it was once argued that white western Europeans were naturally superior to Africans because the former were able to enslave the latter.

There is no such thing out there as a "food chain." It's a concept that we have devised so that we can make our exploitation of animals look as though it has some basis in the natural world. It doesn't. The proclamation that we are at the top of the food chain is equivalent to a proclamation that we are capable of oppressing and exploiting all of the other species on the planet. That may be true but it carries no moral significance.

Are humans different from nonhumans? Certainly. Do humans have abilities that nonhumans lack? Certainly. But animals have all sorts of abilities that humans don't have. Yes, humans can write symphonies (although most don't, by the way). But birds can fly without being in an airplane and fish can breathe under water without an air tank. What, apart from our self-interested proclamation, makes animal abilities worth less as a moral matter than human abilities?

The answer: nothing.

But at the outset, we promised you that we were not going to challenge that bit of conventional wisdom, which holds that although animals matter morally, they don't matter morally as much as humans do. Our conventional wisdom holds that even if animals matter less, they matter *some*, and hurting or killing them requires a justification. Responding to the need for such a justification by saying that we are at the top of some non-existent chain is a way of saying that it's okay to hurt and kill animals without any moral justification.

And that's just a way of saying that you don't think that animals matter at all morally and that we can make them suffer and kill them just because we are able to do so. Actually, if you stop and think about it for a minute, you'll see that our power and ability to exploit nonhuman animals gives us the responsibility to protect them from exploitation!

But... **I know people who consume a vegan diet who are preachy (or hypocritical).**

So do we. On both scores.

So what?

There are people who are advocates for all sorts of moral issues who are preachy — that is, they preach rather than teach. There are also people who advocate for a moral issue, whatever it is, and then engage in what they advise you not to do.

Does either attribute negate the validity of the moral position for which they advocate?

But... Isn't what I eat a matter of my choice?

Consuming animal products is a "choice" only insofar as society allows you to choose to do things that are obviously and indisputably morally wrong. Are you free to choose to hold racist views? Yes. So saying that something is a "choice" says *nothing* about its morality.

We cannot morally justify consuming animal products. Period. Consuming those products may be a matter of "choice" but only in a most superficial sense. It is not a matter of choice for anyone who takes morality seriously. We may be able to choose to harm others but that does not mean that we may, in a moral sense, choose to do so.

To put the matter another way, it does not make sense to say that we think it is morally wrong to inflict unnecessary suffering on animals but then to say that inflicting unnecessary suffering on animals is simply a matter of our choice. We may, in a legal sense, have the freedom to choose to do something that we acknowledge is immoral. But as far as morality is concerned, we don't have a choice.

But... I'm busy and grabbing a quick burger is just more convenient.

Convenience is really no different from pleasure or amusement when it comes to silly excuses if animals matter morally at all.

Another real life example will make the point.

Mitt Romney probably lost the 2012 presidential election at least due in part to what Romney did to Seamus.[34]

Seamus was Romney's Irish setter whom Romney stuck in a crate and strapped to the roof of his station wagon for a 12-hour family trip to Canada in 1983. Seamus apparently defecated, most likely because he was terrified. Romney stopped at a gas station, hosed Seamus down, and stuffed him back into the crate to continue the trip. According to Romney's sons, Seamus ran off when the family got to Canada.

People were outraged about what Romney did to Seamus. We can forgive almost anything but we can't forgive intentionally harming animals without there being a very good reason. To paraphrase a famous quote from Gandhi, "The moral greatness of a presidential wannabe can be judged by the way he treats his dog."

Convenience is not a good reason to inflict suffering on an animal. We got upset with Romney because he just didn't care enough to make sure that Seamus was transported in a safe way in which he was not terrified for hours. Romney let his convenience, his not wanting to be bothered to rent a trailer or a larger vehicle, determine the matter. And that's just not right.

Although anticruelty laws do not do very much, one of the few areas in which they have been used effectively involve situations in which people neglect animals because they simply find it inconvenient to care for them. If you let your dog, horse, or cow starve or die of exposure because you find it too inconvenient to care for the animal, you may well face criminal charges. So what does this tell us?

It tells us that our recognition that animals have some moral value excludes convenience as a rationale for inflicting suffering on animals. Animals matter morally; you cannot make them suffer because you derive pleasure or amusement from doing so, as Vick did, or because you find it convenient, as Romney did.

Animals may not matter much but if they matter at all, our convenience is not a sufficient reason for making them suffer.

This means that you will have to be forced to the burden of opening and warming a can of soup or making a salad instead of eating a burger that is topped with cheese, bacon, and contains more saturated fat and salt than you should consume in a month, as well as served on a bun that contains enough sugar to qualify as a cake. If animals matter at all, and if you have any concern about your health, then ditch the burger.

But... Animals eat other animals.

Our conventional wisdom says that although animals matter morally — and we need to be able to justify imposing suffering and death on them — humans matter more because of characteristics like their ability to engage in moral reasoning and, in a situation of genuine conflict, animals lose and humans win. However, when we are confronted with the fact that our eating animals can't be justified because there is no conflict and we eat animals and animal products simply because we enjoy the taste, we say, "But wait — animals eat each other so why can't we eat them?"

Some animals do, indeed, eat other animals. That's certainly true. But what relevance does that have to the issue of whether we should consume animal products?

That's a rhetorical question; the answer is clear: it has *no* relevance.

First, although some animals eat each other in the wild, many do not. Many animals are vegans. Moreover, there is far more cooperation in nature than what we imagine as the "cruelty of nature."

Second, whether animals eat other animals is beside the point. How is it relevant whether animals eat other animals? Some animals are carnivorous and cannot exist without eating meat. We do not fall into that category; we can get along fine without eating meat and other animal foods, and more and more people are taking the position that our health and environment would both benefit from a shift away from a diet of animal products.

Third, animals do all sorts of things that humans do not regard as morally appropriate. For example, dogs copulate and defecate in the street. Does that mean that we should follow their example or that humans are justified in engaging in the same behaviors?

It is interesting that when it is convenient for us, we attempt to justify our exploitation of animals by resting on our supposed "superiority." And when our supposed "superiority" gets in the way of what we want to do, we suddenly portray ourselves as nothing more than another species of wild animal, as entitled as foxes to eat chickens.

In any event, this argument suffers from the problem that any argument encounters that is of the form, "Doing activity X is morally wrong. But person P is doing X. Therefore it is alright to do X." You can substitute anything for X. Beating up your mother is morally wrong. But wait, John beats up his mother regularly. Therefore, beating up your mother is morally alright."

See the problem?

But... I could never give up [my favorite food].

The sad thing is that this is the "But" we hear most often.

Why is it sad? Well think about it.

We say that animals matter morally and that we should not make them suffer unless we have a good reason. We accept that moral obligation but then ignore the obligation because we find it difficult to give up eating something (meat or dairy products or eggs) that we like.

Would we have any sympathy for Michael Vick if he claimed that he just loved dogfighting and couldn't give it up?

Although we don't think that taste preferences should ever trump serious moral issues and that your love of particular foods should not stand in the way of living a moral life, we should add that there's a vegan substitute for just about any animal food that you think you can't live without. There are vegan versions of meat, cheese (including the kind that melts), and all sorts of vegan milks and ice creams.

But even if there weren't a substitute — even if you had to give up something the taste of which you really liked — can you really say that you value animals morally and that your palate pleasure can trump the interests that animals have in not suffering and dying? For example, dairy products involve not only supporting the veal industry, where most male calves end up, but also the separation of mothers from their babies, sometimes immediately and often after, at most, a day or two after birth. Is that cheese pizza worth it? Is that ice cream worth it? Is that cream in your coffee worth it? There are excellent non-animal alternatives for all of these things. But even if there weren't, or even if you could not afford them or find them where you live, would supporting that terrible industry and the routine practice of taking babies away from their mothers be worth it?

Finally, some people claim to have an "addiction" to cheese and a few in the medical community have endorsed the idea of "cheese addiction." We are very skeptical of this, in part because both of us were significant consumers of cheese at the time we went vegan and although we both missed cheese for a while, neither of us went into "withdrawal" or had anything more than a strong craving for a while. And the overwhelming number of vegans we know will chuckle when hearing about this supposed "addiction." Many of us really liked cheese. But we stopped consuming it because we made a moral decision. Frankly, we think that talking about an "addiction" in this sense is really no different from other strong likes we have, whether it be for cheese (or other foods) or for problematic and immoral behaviors, such as pornography, another thing to which an "addiction" is often claimed. You might crave cheese after you stop eating it. But that's just a desire and it really isn't any different from other desires you have for other things you like.

But... My family and friends will be upset if I stop consuming animal foods.

There are two reactions to this "But": the moral one and the practical one.

The moral response: *why* do you care? Are you going to let the opinion of others prevent you from living in a way that you see as morally right?

Think about it. If you now see that eating animal foods is wrong for the same reason that what Michael Vick did was wrong, why should you care whether others have a negative reaction to your moral thinking? If anything, given that your family members and friends are probably nice people, you might want to discuss with them why they should see the situation in the exact same way.

Presumably, you would not compromise your other moral beliefs for others, so you should not consume animal products in order to make them happy now that you've concluded that our conventional moral thinking rules it out.

Think about this in the context of Michael Vick.

You express to your friend that you are horrified about what Vick did and your friend says that she disagrees and really wants you to attend a dogfight together. Assume that she says that it is really important to her. She's going to get hostile if you don't go.

Would you go to make her happy?

The same analysis applies in the context of eating animal foods or any other activity that you've concluded is morally wrong. You should never do something you think is morally wrong simply because someone else wants you to do so.

The practical response: most people are not going to ask you to go to a dogfight but many of them will react negatively if you don't consume animal products.

Why is this?

The answer is complicated in at least two respects.

First, much of our social life revolves around food and many of our interactions with family and friends have occurred in the context of eating. And, as we mentioned earlier, it is the case that, as a result of habit and absolutely no necessity whatsoever, many people still think that eating means eating animal products; that you haven't had a proper meal if there is no dead animal or animal products on the table. When you announce that you do not consume animal products, you, in effect, excise a primary way in which you have related to that person in the past and you may be worried about how you will relate to that person in the future.

To put the matter another way, you have been eating a dead bird at your grandmother's house for Thanksgiving for the past however many years. You now tell grandma that you aren't eating the bird anymore and will just eat the non-animal foods that she has prepared. You'll be just fine with Brussels sprouts, baked potatoes, salad, etc. She gets upset because she interprets you as saying that even though you're going to be sitting at the table with everyone else, you're not really eating the meal. You're not really having Thanksgiving dinner together. The symbolic function of the meal has been frustrated.

Second, when you inform family and friends that you no longer eat animal foods and that you are doing so because you think that it's morally wrong, what they hear is that you're saying that *they* are immoral people. They take offense.

Their reaction is understandable because, even though the whole issue of eating animals should be as clear as the issue of Michael Vick's dogfighting, it isn't. Eating animal products is culturally pervasive. Most people do it. Most people think it's "normal," and — if normalcy is determined by what most people, at least in rich Western societies, do — it is. You are perceived as announcing an idiosyncratic opinion that is understood as equivalent to saying that you don't eat red apples because you think it's immoral and, what's worse, that you think that anyone who eats red apples is also immoral. It's not just that you're not having Thanksgiving dinner with grandma when you eat only the sprouts, potatoes, and salad; you are telling grandma she's a *bad* person.

For these two practical reasons, it is important to understand that although once you see the immorality of animal use for food because it causes unnecessary suffering, and you see this clearly, the same does not hold true for people who have not yet had that moral perception. It is imperative that you remember this in your interactions with them and help them to have that moral perception by explaining the reasons that have caused you to stop consuming animal products and pointing out they are in agreement with the same conventional moral principles that have led you to your decision.

In other words, you start with Michael Vick.

The idea is not to make judgments about people; the idea is to educate people about how something that they already believe points them in your direction and that it is their inconsistency and not your conduct that is the problem.

But again, the focus is the conduct and discussion about why we do something that most of us think is wrong. The focus is not the moral flaws of the person.

In other words, you don't tell grandma that she's evil. You explain that you're not eating the turkey for the same reason that grandma thinks that dogfighting is wrong. She may not agree with you (at least not from the outset) and be joining you in a Thanksgiving dinner of sprouts, potatoes, and salad, but she'll understand why you're doing it and she'll understand that you are not rejecting or judging her. You're just acting on what we all (including grandma) say we believe: that causing unnecessary suffering is morally wrong.

If you do a gentle but persuasive job educating people, you can deal with negative and even hostile reactions.

But, in the end, you have to ask yourself two simple questions: (1) do I take morality seriously? and (2) am I willing to act on what I claim to take seriously?

Caring about others means that you take the time to explain why you think the way you do and why your conduct is related to moral principles that you share. But caring is *not* doing something you regard as wrong because someone else wants you to do it. So you educate and you explain.

If someone gets hostile and says their happiness is contingent on your doing something that violates your moral beliefs, you need to ask yourself why you would react to that in any way other than sadness.

But... My partner won't go along with it even though I want to.

This is a variant of the preceding "But" but focuses more on the problem of living with someone who doesn't eat the same things you do so that food preparation becomes more complicated as a practical matter.

We have dealt with this "But" a great deal over the years in terms of advising new vegans how to navigate this situation. We offer our thoughts here.

First, in the overwhelming number of cases, the other partner may not be enthusiastic from the outset, but once the moral argument is explained, that person actually does become amenable and sometimes even enthusiastic about switching to a vegan diet. Like all situations in which one person in a relationship has a distinct moral view about an issue, that person has the job of educating the other person. Sometimes, the other person is persuaded, sometimes not. But we know many people who have been persuaded and who consume a vegan diet, at least in the home.

It is imperative that the other partner be educated about, and not bludgeoned with, the moral issue. But that is true of education generally. No one learns if you yell at them or make them feel as though they are morally horrible or stupid. Given the prevalence of the consumption of animal products in our society, many people see a vegan diet as "extreme." Although, as we have discussed and will discuss more later, we think that there are many sensible reasons to reject such a view, the fact remains that it is the dominant view. So we must teach but teach gently.

It is also recommended that the vegan partner endeavor to prepare or provide appetizing vegan meals so that the other partner does not buy into the false notion that vegan food is boring and tasteless. In our experience, partners are usually pleasantly surprised at just how tasty, interesting, and varied vegan food is. They often enjoy sharing in the adventure of exploring many delicious new foods and styles of cuisine. Some of the resources we mention later should help in that regard.

Second, the situation of two (or more) people living together who don't like or eat the same sort of foods is pretty common. If the vegan party does not object to the presence of animal products in the house on moral grounds, the practical problem will be easy to solve. With a minimum amount of effort, most meals can be easily adapted during preparation to cater to both the vegan and non-vegan parties, by, for example, adding tofu or legumes to one portion and meat to the other. It's not necessary to prepare two entirely separate meals.

But... Isn't it difficult and expensive to eat a vegan diet?

No as to both; it is neither difficult nor expensive.

As to difficulty, think fruits, vegetables, beans, grains, nuts, a B-12 source, such as yeast, and a source of essential fatty acids, such as flax or chia seeds, walnuts, or an algae-based supplement. Everything you need to eat a vegan diet is accessible to just about anyone anywhere.

You can spice and prepare these foods just as you spice and prepare animal foods, and people are always amazed at how delicious vegan food is.

If you want processed vegan foods, there are tons. As we mentioned earlier, there are vegan substitutes for meat made of soy, seitan, or other plants; milks (and coffee-friendly creams) made from soy, rice, almond, hemp, or flax; ice creams made from soy, rice, almond, or coconut; and cheeses made of soy, rice, almond, or cashew, including ones that melt for vegan pizza, casseroles, or lasagna.

Many processed vegan foods have high salt content and little nutritive value, just as do processed foods containing animal products. But the processed vegan foods don't have animal fat that will raise your cholesterol and other lipids.

If you need recipes, put "vegan recipes" into any search engine and you will get tens of thousands of recipes. If you want a vegan cookbook, there are hundreds of them. There are books on raw foods, gluten-free foods, and books on foods that are cooked in every conceivable way and in every ethnic cuisine.

Some vegan recipes are involved and time-consuming, just as are some recipes involving animal products. But many are easy and take less than 30 minutes of preparation time.

Some people ask how we can be vegan when we travel. The answer is that it is as easy to get vegan foods just about anywhere. Even if you find yourself somewhere that is extremely heavy on meat and dairy, you can always get a salad with a variety of vegetables and some beans.

But what if you live in places like the Arctic Circle? Believe it or not, when we talk about how easy it is to be vegan, we often get questions like this. The short answer is that they have vegetables, fruits, beans, grains, nuts, and seeds just about everywhere, including the Arctic Circle. We have never gotten this question from anyone who lives at the Arctic Circle or in remote and very cold parts of Canada. But we have been asked this by many people who live in places like New York City or Los Angeles.

Our eating habits are just that — habits. There is nothing inherently difficult about a vegan diet. It just requires that we learn some new habits — not all that many, actually, given that most of us already consume vegetables, fruits, grains, beans, nuts, and seeds. Indeed, the main change of habit going forward concerns what we don't eat any longer and not what we eat to replace those animal foods. And most new vegans are amazed by the wonderful variety of delicious and nutritious foods that they wouldn't have even tried if they had not adopted a vegan diet!

What about information about nutrition for those on a

vegan diet? There are many sources. We find Joel Fuhrman, M.D. (www.DrFuhrman.com) to be comprehensive, reliable, and accessible. Dr. Fuhrman is a physician and lifelong vegan who has dealt with just about every nutritional issue imaginable. Additionally, our website www.HowDoIGoVegan.com contains nutritional information and a wide variety of easy and delicious recipes.

There is some idea out there that if you decide to stop eating animal products, you are going to have to go live on a hippy commune (if you could find one) and start growing and preparing all your own food.

That's just plain silly. If you decide to adopt a vegan diet right now, you can learn everything you need to know to make a successful start in two hours and be on your way.

As for expense, a diet of fruits, vegetables, beans, grains, nuts, and seeds is cheaper than a diet that includes meat, dairy, and eggs. In most cases, a vegan diet will be much cheaper. Processed vegan foods are sometimes pricey, but a package of soy burgers is usually no more expensive, and is often less expensive, than a comparable quantity of meat. And, as we mentioned above, processed foods, whether vegan or animal-based, are not particularly healthy things to consume.

Some people will point out that organic vegetables and fruits are often more expensive than animal foods. That may be true in some cases, but organic plant foods are certainly no more expensive, and, indeed, are far less expensive, than organic animal foods — and that is the proper standard of comparison.

Finally, some people claim that it is "elitist" to eat a vegan diet. We're not sure what they mean by this. As we've said, a diet of plant foods is invariably cheaper than a diet that includes animal foods. And many people in the world who are anything but affluent consume a diet of all or substantially all plant foods. In any event, whatever is meant by characterizing a vegan diet as "elitist," we would suggest that there is *nothing* more elitist than the idea that our palate pleasure can justify imposing suffering and death on a sentient being who values her or his life as much as we do ours.

But... **I'm too old to change.**

You're never too old to do something that you think you should do and your age can never be an acceptable excuse.

Think about an analogy involving human rights: would anyone who had concluded that racism is immoral say, "But I'm too old to change?"

If you think that it is morally wrong to participate in the unnecessary suffering and death of animals, then you have to act on that moral belief just as you would any other. Besides, as we have explained, it's not at all difficult to remove meat, dairy, and eggs from your diet.

But... I'm too young to change.

This "But" is often articulated by young people, usually minors, who are still living in their parents' home and when their parents are concerned that a vegan diet will not be nutritious. This is another situation with which we have had a fair amount of experience.

The reputable information widely available, which we have mentioned earlier, is quite clear: a sensible vegan diet is at least as healthy as a diet that includes animal foods, and many respected health-care professionals agree that it's even *more* healthy. So kids who are wannabe vegans can provide their parents with a wealth of information that should dispel all of the myths about a vegan diet as well as address any specific concerns that parents have.

There are, of course, some parents who object to this sort of change not because they are concerned about health but because they think it's just odd, or because they don't like their children being different, particularly in ways that they aren't different, or because they think that their child is just going through a phase. Although we would think that parents would be delighted that their child was thinking about any moral issue in a serious way — given that many children do not think about any such issues because mainstream media goes out of its way to ensure they don't — we accept that some parents may object on non-health grounds. All we can say is that some children just have to confront the fact that they are more morally advanced than their parents are, and will have to wait until they go off to college (where it's easy to eat vegan) or until they otherwise leave home.

If the objection by the parents is the extra time and work involved in preparing separate meals, the young person may want to learn to cook for herself or himself. They might also consider, for example, making a vegan meal for the whole family once a week. This is a way of educating their family about nutritious and appealing vegan food and at the same time giving their parents a welcome break from food preparation. There are very few parents who would object to this!

But... What if I can't give up all animal foods right away?

Of course you can!

As we explained in the previous section, switching to a vegan diet is a piece of (vegan) cake! We are telling you right now — you *can* do it!

If, however, the idea is overwhelming to you even though it should not be, we recommend that you approach it by switching to a vegan diet in four easy steps.

Go vegan for breakfast for a week, or two weeks, or for however long you need to assure yourself you can do it, it's easy, and that you won't die, or go blind, or whatever. Breakfast is super easy for vegan foods.

And then go vegan for lunch for some period of time.

And then go vegan for dinner for some period of time.

And then go vegan for all snacks.

And now you have a completely vegan diet.

But... Isn't eating more "humanely" produced animal foods a good first step?

No.

Let's assume you have concluded that you are troubled by eating animal foods. What we strongly *don't* recommend is that, in response to this, you decide as an "interim" measure to consume "happy" meat from animals supposedly raised or killed "humanely;" or "happy" milk from cows who were supposedly treated with "compassion;" or eggs from hens who were in larger "enriched" cages or in one large cage called a "cage-free" barn.

Our opposition to "happy" animal products is not only that we think that these "improvements" aren't really improvements at all and are, as we discussed earlier, really similar to putting padding on a waterboard at Guantanamo Bay. Our opposition is that this "solution" makes no sense given the conventional wisdom we claim to accept.

That is, although we think these "improvements" do very little if anything, what if they did do something? What if they reduced overall animal suffering by 50% or 80%? It would be beyond absurd to claim anything like that but let's assume for the sake of argument that it was accurate.

So what?

Let's consider an example involving humans. We all agree that it is wrong to inflict unnecessary suffering on children. We all agree that it would be morally horrible to inflict suffering on children for reasons of pleasure because that would be completely unnecessary under *anyone's* views about what constitutes appropriate discipline for children. That is, even if you think it's okay to spank a child under some circumstances, no one thinks it's acceptable to spank a child for pleasure.

Assume that John and Mary spank their child severely for pleasure. You are horrified at this. Assume that either because the authorities don't care, which, despite what we'd like to believe, is often the case in many places, or because John and Mary will lie convincingly to the authorities and claim that the child misbehaved and merited the spanking, you decide to intervene and talk with John and Mary.

They agree with you but their solution is to use a softer belt or to reduce the number of blows by half or more.

Is that better?

Yes, sure it is.

Is it *right?*

Absolutely not.

As a matter of economic reality, the idea that we will *ever* reduce the suffering of the billions of animals used for food by 50% or even 20% or 30% is — and we mean this very literally — on a par with a belief in Santa Claus. It's *fantasy*. Period.

But even if we could reduce it by 50% or more, would it be right given that we — you — believe that it's wrong to inflict unnecessary suffering on animals?

Absolutely not.

Therefore, if you really believe what you say you believe — that animals matter morally but humans matter more and that animals lose in any real conflict — your obligation is crystal clear: you cannot justify any suffering imposed on animals used for food and you are obligated to adopt a vegan diet.

But... Isn't going vegetarian a good first step?

No.

As we've said above, there is no morally coherent distinction between meat and other animal products. Dairy and eggs also involve suffering and death. In fact, if you stop eating beef and get the same number of calories from eggs, you may actually be responsible for more animal suffering and death given that laying hens are usually killed after one or two laying cycles and all the male chicks born to laying hens are killed immediately.

In any event, the meat, dairy, and egg industries are inextricably intertwined. They all necessarily involve suffering; they all necessarily involve death. To stop eating meat but to continue to eat dairy is morally arbitrary and similar to a decision to stop eating meat from spotted cows but to continue to eat meat from brown cows. It makes no sense.

Consumption of any animal products — absent your being stranded on a desert island or adrift on a lifeboat, with no plant foods available — is *completely* inconsistent with the conventional wisdom we claim to accept.

As we discussed above, the good first step is not consuming "happy" animal products or making an arbitrary distinction between meat and other animal products and not eating the former but continuing to eat the latter. The good first step, if you don't feel able to go vegan immediately, is to do it in stages, starting with breakfast and continuing on.

But... **If I accept that I can't continue to eat meat and other animal products, am I committed to rejecting all animal use for any purpose?**

Now you have been confronted with the argument that given what you say you believe, you're committed to not eating animals or animal products because their production invariably involves suffering and our best justification for imposing that suffering or causing it to be imposed is that animal flesh and animal products taste good.

The argument troubled you so you started thinking about all of those "But" points that you've relied on over the years to avoid coming to this conclusion sooner. But then you read the foregoing and you now have to acknowledge something else you've known all along — that the "Buts" are, for the most, pretty silly. So now you're really considering that the whole vegan thing isn't as extreme as you once thought.

But wait.

If you take this step — if you stop eating animal products — where is this going to lead you? Can you still wear leather, or wool, or fur? Are you now obligated to stop attending circuses? Are you obligated to oppose the use animals in experiments or in product testing?

That is a discussion for another day.

In this discussion, we are focusing on one and only one thing: if you think that Michael Vick did wrong when he engaged in animal fighting, you can't justify eating animal foods. If you think that animals matter at all morally, you cannot, without being a hypocrite, continue to support suffering and death that is every bit as frivolous as what Michael Vick did.

Period.

That's all we're talking about here.

We can, however, assure you that if you accept the argument we are making, and you stop eating animal products, we think it will be clear to you as to where you go from there as it concerns others issues.

If you want to explore the ethical dimension of animal use in greater depth, as well as obtain practical information on how to be vegan, we invite you to visit our websites:

www.AbolitionistApproach.com

www.HowDoIGoVegan.com

* * *

In sum, we've examined all of the major "Buts" that we use to keep ourselves from seeing that there is no difference between what Michael Vick did and what the rest of us do.

None of these "Buts" works. All buts are off the table, so to speak. We just need to get the animals and animal products off the table as well.

III. Conclusion

Having read this far, you either agree with us, and you acknowledge that you are obligated to adopt a vegan diet, or you don't agree with us because you have concluded that you don't really think that animals matter morally, or because you think that they matter morally but that you still aren't going to change your behavior, and you are willing to live with what is a serious moral inconsistency.

In any event, you don't need us to draw any conclusions for you.

If, however, you have decided that you are going to put your morality where your mouth is and adopt a vegan diet, we want to offer some advice: in a society in which most people consume animal products and where conformity is valued, and in which non-conforming behavior is often dismissed as "extreme," you will inevitably find others labeling you as "extreme."

Don't let that bother you. Consider:

What is extreme is eating decomposing flesh, milk produced for the young of another species, and the unfertilized eggs of birds.

What is extreme is that we regard some animals as members of our family while, at the same time, we stick forks into the corpses of other animals.

What is extreme is thinking that it is morally acceptable to inflict suffering and death on other sentient creatures simply because we enjoy the taste of animal products.

What is extreme is that we say we recognize that "unnecessary" suffering and death cannot be morally justified and then we proceed to engage in exploitation on a daily basis that is completely unnecessary.

What is extreme is that we excoriate people like Michael Vick while we continue to eat animal products.

What is extreme is pretending to embrace peace while we make violence, suffering, torture, and death a daily part of our lives.

What is extreme is that we say we care about animals and we believe that they are members of the moral community, but we sponsor, support, encourage and promote "happy" meat/dairy labeling schemes.

What is extreme is not eating flesh but continuing to consume dairy when there is absolutely no rational distinction between meat and dairy (or other animal products). There is as much suffering and death in dairy, eggs, etc., as there is in meat.

What is extreme is that we are consuming a diet that is causing disease and resulting in ecological disaster.

What is extreme is that we encourage our children to love animals at the same time we teach them that those whom they love can also be those whom they harm. We teach our children that loving others is consistent with hurting them. That is truly extreme — and very sad.

What is extreme is the fantasy that we will ever find our moral compass with respect to animals as long as they are on our tables.

What is extreme is that we say we care about animals but we continue to eat animals and animal products.

For Further Reading

On animal ethics

Books

Gary L. Francione:

The Animal Rights Debate: Abolition or Regulation? (with Robert Garner) (Columbia University Press 2010);

Animals as Persons: Essays on the Abolition of Animal Exploitation (Columbia University Press 2008);

Introduction to Animal Rights: Your Child or the Dog? (Temple University Press 2000)

Gary Steiner:

Animals and the Moral Community: Mental Life, Moral Status, and Kinship (Columbia University Press 2008)

Online resources

www.AbolitionistApproach.com

www.HowDoIGoVegan.com

www.facebook.com/abolitionistapproach

www.twitter.com/garyfrancione

www.youtube.com/channel/UC_qKzDKiOkCjkz0JKl1BufA

On nutrition and medical topics

We find Joel Fuhrman, M.D. to be the single most reliable source of nutritional and medical information relating to a plant-based diet. Dr. Fuhrman approaches the issue from a health perspective and not from the perspective of animal ethics. You can find his books and other educational materials at www.DrFuhrman.com.

On practical information about veganism

Our website www.HowDoIGoVegan.com will orient you in terms of the practical aspects of going vegan, not just with respect to diet, but also with respect to eliminating animal use as much as possible from all other aspects of your life. Additionally, this resource will help you understand veganism according to the perspective of animal ethics that we have developed over the years, which we refer to as the Abolitionist Approach to Animal Rights.

About the Authors

Gary L. Francione is Board of Governors Distinguished Professor of Law and the Nicholas deB. Katzenbach Scholar of Law and Philosophy at Rutgers University School of Law.

Anna Charlton is Adjunct Professor of Law at Rutgers University School of Law. She was the co-founder and co-director (with Gary L. Francione) of the Rutgers Animal Rights Law Clinic from 1990-2000.

Endnotes

[1] See, e.g., Academy of Nutrition and Dietetics
(http://www.eatrightpro.org/resource/practice/position-and-
practice-papers/position-papers/vegetarian-diets); American
Diabetes Association (http://www.diabetes.org/food-and-
fitness/food/planning-meals/meal-planning-for-vegetarians/);
American Heart Association;
(http://www.heart.org/HEARTORG/GettingHealthy/Nutrition
Center/Vegetarian-Diets_UCM_306032_Article.jsp); British
Dietetic Association
(http://www.bda.uk.com/foodfacts/vegetarianfoodfacts.pdf);
British National Health Service
(http://www.nhs.uk/Livewell/Vegetarianhealth/Pages/Vegandiet
s.aspx); British Nutrition Foundation
(http://www.nutrition.org.uk/publications/briefingpapers/vegeta
rian-nutrition); Dietary Guidelines of the U.S. Department of
Agriculture and U.S. Department of Health and Human Services
(http://health.gov/dietaryguidelines/2010/); Dieticians
Association of Australia (http://daa.asn.au/for-the-public/smart-
eating-for-you/nutrition-a-z/vegan-diets/); Dieticians of Canada
(http://www.dietitians.ca/Your-Health/Nutrition-A-
Z/Vegetarian-Diets/Eating-Guidelines-for-Vegans.aspx); Heart
and Stroke Foundation
(http://www.heartandstroke.com/site/c.ikIQLcMWJtE/b.34842
49/k.2F6C/Healthy_living__Vegetarian_diets.htm); Kaiser
Permanente
(http://www.thepermanentejournal.org/issues/2013/spring/5117
-nutrition.html); Mayo Clinic
(http://www.mayoclinic.org/healthy-lifestyle/nutrition-and-
healthy-eating/in-depth/vegetarian-diet/art-20046446); National
Institutes for Health
(https://www.nlm.nih.gov/medlineplus/vegetariandiet.html);

University of California (Los Angeles) Medical Center
(http://www.dining.ucla.edu/housing_site/dining/SNAC_pdf/V
egetarianism.pdf); University of Pennsylvania School of Medicine
(http://www.pennmedicine.org/encyclopedia/em_DisplayArticle.
aspx?gcid=002465&); University of Pittsburgh Medical Center
(http://www.upmc.com/health-
library/Pages/HealthwiseIndex.aspx?qid=abq2485).

2 David Pimentel and Marcia Pimentel, "Sustainability of meat-
based and plant-based diets and the environment," *American
Journal of Clinical Nutrition* 2003; 78 (suppl): 660S-3S, available at
http://ajcn.nutrition.org/content/78/3/660S.full.pdf

3 Institution of Mechanical Engineers, *Global Food: Waste Not,
Want Not* (2013), at 12, available at:
http://www.imeche.org/docs/default-
source/reports/Global_Food_Report.pdf?sfvrsn=0

4 FAO Newsroom,
http://www.fao.org/newsroom/en/news/2006/1000448/

5 See Pimentel study.

6 Pew Commission on Industrial Farm Animal Production, at
http://www.ncifap.org/issues/environment/

7 See Natural Resources Defense Council, at
http://www.nrdc.org/food/saving-antibiotics.asp

8 Patrick Barkham, "Cat bin woman Mary Bale fined £250," *The
Guardian*, Oct. 19, 2010, at
http://www.guardian.co.uk/world/2010/oct/19/cat-bin-woman-
mary-bale

9 See Nicholas Graham, "Julio Aparicio GORED IN THROAT
During Bullfight," in *Huffington Post*, May 22, 2010, at

http://www.huffingtonpost.com/2010/05/22/julio-aparicio-gored-in-t_n_585941.html

[10] Joel Fuhrman, M.D., *Eat to Live* (Little Brown and Company 2011), at 184.

[11] James Gallagher, "Iodine deficiency 'may lower UK children's IQ,'" BBC News, May 22, 2013, at http://www.bbc.co.uk/news/health-22607161

[12] *Genesis* 1:29 (all references are to King James Bible).

[13] *Genesis* 1:30.

[14] *Genesis* 9:3.

[15] *Isaiah* 2:4.

[16] *Isaiah* 65:25.

[17] See *Genesis* 19:1-8.

[18] See *Leviticus* 19:27.

[19] See *Leviticus* 19:28.

[20] See *Leviticus* 19:19.

[21] See *Leviticus* 15:19-30; 20:18; *Ezekiel* 18:5-6

[22] See *I Corinthians* 14:34-35.

[23] See *Deuteronomy* 23:1.

[24] See *Deuteronomy* 25:11-12.

[25] See *Exodus* 21:17.

26 Rob Dunn, "Human Ancestors Were Nearly All Vegetarians," *Scientific American Guest Blog,* July 23, 2012, at http://blogs.scientificamerican.com/guest-blog/2012/07/23/human-ancestors-were-nearly-all-vegetarians/

27 See Major Crops Grown in the United States, at http://www.epa.gov/oecaagct/ag101/cropmajor.html

28 Worldwatch Institute, "Is Meat Sustainable?," at http://www.worldwatch.org/node/549 (quoting U.S. Department of Commerce, Census of Agriculture).

29 See Alex Kirby, "Fish do feel pain, scientists say," *BBC News,* April 30, 2003, at http://news.bbc.co.uk/1/hi/sci/tech/2983045.stm

30 *Acaranga Sutra,* at 1.4.1.

31 Donald R Griffin *Animal Minds: Beyond Cognition to Consciousness* (University of Chicago Press 2001), at 274.

32 Gareth Cook, "Do Plants Think?" *Scientific American,* June 5, 2012, at http://www.scientificamerican.com/article.cfm?id=do-plants-think-daniel-chamovitz

33 "Michael Marder and Gary Francione Debate Plant Ethics," Columbia University Press Website, at http://www.cupblog.org/?p=6604

34 Gary L. Francione, "Thinking About Mitt Romney and Seamus, Michael Vick and Dog Fighting, and Eating Animals," April 18, 2012, at http://truth-out.org/news/item/8459-thinking-about-mitt-romney-and-seamus-michael-vick-and-dog-fighting-and-eating-animals

Made in the USA
Monee, IL
22 August 2022